A HANDBOOK FOR
High Reliability Schools™

••• The Next Step in School Reform

ROBERT J. MARZANO
PHILIP B. WARRICK
JULIA A. SIMMS

With
David Livingston
Pam Livingston
Fred Pleis
Tammy Heflebower
Jan K. Hoegh
Sonny Magaña

MARZANO
—Research—

555 North Morton Street
Bloomington, IN 47404
888.849.0851
FAX: 866.801.1447
email: info@marzanoresearch.com
marzanoresearch.com

Printed in the United States of America

Library of Congress Control Number: 2014905526

ISBN: 978-0-9833512-7-6 (paperback)

Text and Cover Designer: Rian Anderson
Compositor: Rachel Smith

Marzano Research Development Team

Visit **marzanoresearch.com/reproducibles/leadership**
to access online-only reproducibles and live links from this book.
Visit **marzanoresearch.com/HRSNetwork** to learn more about the HRS Network.

Table of Contents

Italicized entries indicate reproducibles.

About the Authors ix

About Marzano Research xiii

Introduction
Ushering in the New Era of School Reform 1

    Creating High Reliability Schools 1

        A Hierarchy of School Factors 2

        Leading and Lagging Indicators 4

    Implementing Critical Commitments 6

    Monitoring Performance for Continuous Improvement 6

        Quick Data 8

        Problem Prevention and Celebration of Success 10

        Level-Appropriate Data Collection 11

    Overview of the Model 11

    How to Use This Book 12

Chapter 1
Safe and Collaborative Culture 15

    Level 1 Short-Form Leading Indicator Survey 15

    Level 1 Long-Form Leading Indicator Surveys 16

    Reproducible 1.1: Level 1 Long-Form Leading Indicator Survey for Teachers and Staff 17

    Reproducible 1.2: Level 1 Long-Form Leading Indicator Survey for Administrators 20

    Reproducible 1.3: Level 1 Long-Form Leading Indicator Survey for Students 23

    Reproducible 1.4: Level 1 Long-Form Leading Indicator Survey for Parents 24

    Level 1 Critical Commitment 27

    Level 1 Lagging Indicators 28

        Example 1 29

        Example 2 31

        Example 3 32

Quick Data for Level 1 33

    Quick Conversations 33

    Quick Observations 33

    Easy-to-Collect Quantitative Data 34

    Acknowledging and Celebrating Success 34

Resources for Level 1 35

Chapter 2
Effective Teaching in Every Classroom 37

Level 2 Short-Form Leading Indicator Survey 37

Level 2 Long-Form Leading Indicator Surveys 38

Reproducible 2.1: Level 2 Long-Form Leading Indicator Survey for Teachers and Staff 39

Reproducible 2.2: Level 2 Long-Form Leading Indicator Survey for Administrators 41

Reproducible 2.3: Level 2 Long-Form Leading Indicator Survey for Students 43

Reproducible 2.4: Level 2 Long-Form Leading Indicator Survey for Parents 44

Level 2 Critical Commitment 46

    The System Is Comprehensive and Specific 46

    The System Includes a Developmental Scale 49

    The System Acknowledges and Supports Growth 50

Level 2 Lagging Indicators 50

    Example 1 51

    Example 2 52

    Example 3 53

Quick Data for Level 2 53

    Quick Conversations 53

    Quick Observations 54

    Easy-to-Collect Quantitative Data 54

    Acknowledging and Celebrating Success 55

Resources for Level 2 56

Chapter 3
Guaranteed and Viable Curriculum 57

Level 3 Short-Form Leading Indicator Survey 57

Level 3 Long-Form Leading Indicator Surveys 58

Reproducible 3.1: Level 3 Long-Form Leading Indicator Survey for Teachers and Staff 59

Reproducible 3.2: Level 3 Long-Form Leading Indicator Survey for Administrators 62

Reproducible 3.3: Level 3 Long-Form Leading Indicator Survey for Students 65

Reproducible 3.4: Level 3 Long-Form Leading Indicator Survey for Parents 67

Level 3 Critical Commitments 69

    Continually Monitor the Viability of the Curriculum 70

    Create a Comprehensive Vocabulary Program 70

    Use Direct Instruction in Knowledge Application and Metacognitive Skills 73

Level 3 Lagging Indicators 75

    Example 1 76

    Example 2 77

    Example 3 78

Quick Data for Level 3 78

    Quick Conversations 78

    Quick Observations 79

    Easy-to-Collect Quantitative Data 80

    Acknowledging and Celebrating Success 80

Resources for Level 3 81

Chapter 4

Standards-Referenced Reporting 83

Level 4 Short-Form Leading Indicator Survey 83

Level 4 Long-Form Leading Indicator Surveys 84

Reproducible 4.1: Level 4 Long-Form Leading Indicator Survey for Teachers and Staff 85

Reproducible 4.2: Level 4 Long-Form Leading Indicator Survey for Administrators 86

Reproducible 4.3: Level 4 Long-Form Leading Indicator Survey for Students 87

Reproducible 4.4: Level 4 Long-Form Leading Indicator Survey for Parents 88

Level 4 Critical Commitments 89

    Develop Proficiency Scales for the Essential Content 89

    Report Status and Growth on the Report Card Using Proficiency Scales 91

Level 4 Lagging Indicators 94

    Example 1 96

    Example 2 96

    Example 3 97

Quick Data for Level 4 97

    Quick Conversations 97

    Quick Observations 98

    Easy-to-Collect Quantitative Data 98

    Acknowledging and Celebrating Success 98

Resources for Level 4 99

Chapter 5

Competency-Based Education 101

Level 5 Short-Form Leading Indicator Survey 101

Level 5 Long-Form Leading Indicator Surveys 102

Reproducible 5.1: Level 5 Long-Form Leading Indicator Survey for Teachers and Staff 103

Reproducible 5.2: Level 5 Long-Form Leading Indicator Survey for Administrators 104

Reproducible 5.3: Level 5 Long-Form Leading Indicator Survey for Students 105

Reproducible 5.4: Level 5 Long-Form Leading Indicator Survey for Parents 106

Level 5 Critical Commitments 107

    Get Rid of Time Requirements 107

    Adjust Reporting Systems Accordingly 108

Level 5 Lagging Indicators 112

    Example 1 113

    Example 2 114

    Example 3 115

Quick Data for Level 5 115

    Quick Conversations 115

    Quick Observations 116

    Easy-to-Collect Quantitative Data 116

    Acknowledging and Celebrating Success 117

Resources for Level 5 117

Epilogue **119**

Guideline 1: Provide a General Overview of the High Reliability Process to Teachers, Staff, and Administrators 119

Guideline 2: Select Leading and Lagging Indicators That Are Appropriate for Your School 120

Guideline 3: Work on Levels 1, 2, and 3 Simultaneously, but Seek High Reliability Status for One Level at a Time 120

Guideline 4: If Necessary, Set Interim Criterion Scores for Lagging Indicators 121

Guideline 5: Lead From the Perspective of the Indicators 121

References and Resources **123**

Index **131**

About the Authors

Robert J. Marzano, PhD, is the cofounder and CEO of Marzano Research in Denver, Colorado. During his forty years in the field of education, he has worked with educators as a speaker and trainer and has authored more than thirty books and 150 articles on topics such as instruction, assessment, writing and implementing standards, cognition, effective leadership, and school intervention. His books include *The Art and Science of Teaching*, *Leaders of Learning*, *On Excellence in Teaching*, *Effective Supervision*, *The Classroom Strategies Series*, *Using Common Core Standards to Enhance Classroom Instruction and Assessment*, *Vocabulary for the Common Core*, and *Teacher Evaluation That Makes a Difference*. His practical translations of the most current research and theory into classroom strategies are known internationally and are widely practiced by both teachers and administrators. He received a bachelor's degree from Iona College in New York, a master's degree from Seattle University, and a doctorate from the University of Washington.

Philip B. Warrick, EdD, is an associate vice president of Marzano Research. He was an award-winning administrator for nearly twelve years, most recently as principal of Round Rock High School, which serves nearly three thousand students. Phil has been an adjunct professor at Peru State College since 2005. In 2010, he was invited to participate in the Texas Principals' Visioning Institute, where he worked with other principals to develop model practices for Texas schools. He is a former regional president for the Nebraska Council of School Administrators (NCSA). He also served on the NCSA legislative committee and was elected chair. In 2003, he was one of the first participants to attend the Nebraska Educational Leadership Institute, conducted by the Gallup Corporation at Gallup University in Omaha. Phil was named Nebraska Outstanding New Principal of the Year and Nebraska Secondary School Principals Region One Assistant Principal of the Year in 1998, Nebraska Secondary School Principals Region One Principal of the Year in 2004, and Nebraska State High School Principal of the Year in 2005. He earned a bachelor of science from Chadron State College and master's and doctoral degrees from the University of Nebraska–Lincoln.

Julia A. Simms, EdM, MA, is director of publications for Marzano Research in Denver, Colorado. She has worked in K–12 education as a classroom teacher, gifted education specialist, teacher leader, and coach. Her books include *Coaching Classroom Instruction, Using Common Core Standards to Enhance Classroom Instruction and Assessment, Vocabulary for the Common Core,* and *Questioning Sequences in the Classroom.* She has led school- and district-level professional development on a variety of topics, including literacy instruction and intervention, classroom and schoolwide differentiation, and instructional technology. She received her bachelor's degree from Wheaton College in Wheaton, Illinois, and master's degrees in educational administration and K–12 literacy from Colorado State University and the University of Northern Colorado, respectively.

David Livingston, PhD, specializes in school- and district-level leadership and school improvement. He was a teacher for ten years, a principal (of four different elementary schools) for twenty years, and executive director of elementary education for the Cherry Creek School District in Colorado for eight years. David has also been coordinator for the Western States Benchmarking Consortium, an adjunct professor at the University of Colorado Denver, and a member of the board of trustees for Stanley British Primary School (also in Denver). David holds a doctorate in history and philosophy of education from the University of Colorado Boulder and a master's degree in urban education from Roosevelt University. He began teaching with the Teacher Corps in 1968 after graduating from Wheaton College with a bachelor's degree in literature.

Pam Livingston, MA, has fourteen years of experience as a classroom teacher and staff developer and seventeen years as a building administrator. Before becoming a principal, she was a professional development specialist in early childhood education at Cherry Creek Schools in Colorado, where she facilitated the study and development of curriculum and assessments for young children and guided professional development for primary teachers. Her elementary school received the 2011 Colorado Commissioner's Choice Award for Teacher Leadership. Pam's leadership experiences include principalships at a large suburban school district and a small mountain community, as well as in schools serving low- to high-socioeconomic neighborhoods. Pam received a bachelor's degree and a master's degree in early childhood education from the University of Northern Colorado and completed an educational administration program at the University of Colorado Denver.

Fred Pleis, EdM, is the Marzano High Reliability Schools™ implementation manager for Marzano Research in Denver, Colorado. He oversees planning, development, and facilitation as schools implement the Marzano High Reliability Schools model. He has worked in K–12 education as a classroom teacher, leadership team member, and athletic coach. Fred has presented at multiple conferences and has been a school leader for professional learning communities and response to intervention. Fred received his bachelor's degree in early childhood and elementary education from Temple University in Philadelphia, Pennsylvania, and his master's degree in educational leadership from Regis University in Denver, Colorado.

Tammy Heflebower, EdD, is a senior scholar at Marzano Research with experience working in urban, rural, and suburban districts throughout North America, Europe, Canada, and Australia. She has served as a classroom teacher, building-level leader, district leader, regional professional development director, and national trainer and as an adjunct professor of curriculum, instruction, and assessment at several universities. Tammy received the District Distinguished Teacher Award and worked as a national educational trainer for the National Resource and Training Center at Boys Town in Nebraska. She also served as director of curriculum, instruction, and assessment at Douglas County School District in Colorado and as a leader of many statewide organizations in Nebraska and Colorado. Tammy has coauthored several articles and the book *Teaching & Assessing 21st Century Skills* and is a contributor to *Becoming a Reflective Teacher*, *The Highly Engaged Classroom*, *Using Common Core Standards to Enhance Classroom Instruction and Assessment*, and *Coaching Classroom Instruction*. Tammy holds a bachelor of arts from Hastings College in Nebraska (where she was honored as an Outstanding Young Alumna), a master of arts from the University of Nebraska Omaha, and a doctor of education in educational administration and an educational administrative endorsement from the University of Nebraska–Lincoln.

Jan K. Hoegh, MA, is an associate vice president of Marzano Research. She is a former classroom teacher, professional development specialist, assistant high school principal, and curriculum coordinator. Jan, who has twenty-eight years of experience in education, also served as assistant director of statewide assessment for the Nebraska Department of Education, where her primary focus was Nebraska State Accountability test development. She has served on numerous statewide and national standards and assessment committees and has presented at national conferences. An active member of several educational organizations, Jan was president of the Nebraska Association for Supervision and Curriculum Development. She is a member of the Association for Supervision and Curriculum Development and Nebraska Council of School Administrators. Jan holds a bachelor of arts in elementary education and a master of arts in educational administration, both from the University of Nebraska at Kearney. She also earned a specialization in assessment from the University of Nebraska–Lincoln.

Anthony J. "Sonny" Magaña, EdM, is an associate vice president of Marzano Research and director of the educational technology division. He works with teams of teachers and leaders to support, enhance, and expand powerful instructional strategies with technology. Sonny has served in the field of education for thirty years as a classroom teacher, building principal, district administrator, state technology project director, speaker, and trainer. He coauthored *Enhancing the Art and Science of Teaching With Technology*. Sonny created and served as director of Washington's first CyberSchool, a successful blended learning program that continues to meet the needs of at-risk students in Washington State. He received the Milken National Educator Award in 1997 and the Governor's Commendation for Distinguished Achievement in Education in 1998. Sonny received a bachelor of science degree in biology from Stockton College in New Jersey and a master's degree in educational technology from City University of Seattle. He is completing a doctorate at Seattle University.

About Marzano Research

Marzano Research is a joint venture between Solution Tree and Dr. Robert J. Marzano. Marzano Research combines Dr. Marzano's forty years of educational research with continuous action research in all major areas of schooling in order to provide effective and accessible instructional strategies, leadership strategies, and classroom assessment strategies that are always at the forefront of best practice. By providing such an all-inclusive research-into-practice resource center, Marzano Research provides teachers and principals the tools they need to effect profound and immediate improvement in student achievement.

Introduction

Ushering in the New Era of School Reform

• • •

In industries where mistakes and errors lead to significant and far-reaching consequences—such as nuclear power plants, air traffic control towers, and electrical power grids—organizations must adjust their operations to proactively prevent failure. G. Thomas Bellamy, Lindy Crawford, Laura Marshall, and Gail Coulter (2005) reviewed the literature on these high reliability organizations (HROs) and explained that "what distinguishes HROs is not the absence of errors but the ability to contain their effects so they do not escalate into significant failures" (p. 385). Bellamy and his colleagues further commented,

> The literature on HROs describes how organizations operate when accidents or failures are simply too significant to be tolerated, where failures make headlines. . . . The study of HROs has evolved through empirical investigation of catastrophic accidents, near misses, and organizations that succeed despite very trying and dangerous circumstances. Launched by Perrow's (1984) analysis of the nuclear accident at Three Mile Island, the literature evolved through discussions of whether such accidents are inevitable, as Perrow suggested, or might be avoided through strategies used by organizations that operate successfully in high-risk conditions (Bierly & Spender, 1995; Roberts, 1990). (p. 385)

Karl Weick, Kathleen Sutcliffe, and David Obstfeld (1999) described HROs as organizations that "take a variety of extraordinary steps in pursuit of error-free performance" (p. 84). More recently, Weick and Sutcliffe (2007) observed that "HROs work hard to anticipate and specify significant mistakes that they don't want to make. Ongoing attention to these potentially significant failures is built into their practices" (p. 53). These organizations have instituted systems, procedures, and processes that allow them to minimize failures and quickly address or remedy them if they do occur. In other words, the public can rely on these organizations not to make mistakes and to resolve them quickly when they do occur.

Schools are not typically thought of as high reliability organizations. However, nothing prevents a school from becoming an organization that takes proactive steps to prevent failure and ensure success.

Creating High Reliability Schools

A high reliability school, by definition, monitors the effectiveness of critical factors within the system and immediately takes action to contain the negative effects of any errors that occur. As early as 1995, Sam Stringfield called for the development of high reliability schools. He and his colleagues later described schools that operate as high reliability organizations (Stringfield, Reynolds, & Schaffer, 2008, 2012). These schools have several things in common, including high, clear, shared goals; real-time, understandable, comprehensive data systems; collaborative environments; flexibility; formalized operating procedures; a focus on best practices and expertise over seniority; rigorous teacher performance evaluations; and clean, well-functioning campuses.

what we need

To implement this type of a high reliability perspective in schools, two elements are necessary: (1) a hierarchy of school factors and (2) leading and lagging indicators.

A Hierarchy of School Factors

From the 1950s to the 1980s, public education in the United States experienced a wave of pessimism regarding its potential to positively impact student achievement (Coleman et al., 1966; Jencks et al., 1972; National Commission on Excellence in Education, 1983; Rickover, 1959). Many condemned schools, saying they "bring little influence to bear on a child's achievement that is independent of his background and general social context" (Coleman et al., 1966, p. 325). Although this criticism shed light on areas of weakness in the U.S. public education system, the conclusion that schools have no effect on student achievement is not valid for at least three reasons.

schools do make an impact

First, much of the research used to support the perspective that schools fail to impact students positively can be interpreted in alternative ways, some of which indicate that schools *can* cultivate high levels of student achievement. Second, there are many examples of highly effective schools that have successfully overcome the effects of students' backgrounds. Third, and perhaps most importantly, school effectiveness research paints an optimistic picture of schools' ability to impact student achievement. In fact, the aggregated research (including the following studies) indicates that there are clear, specific, and concrete actions that schools can take to dramatically increase their effectiveness.

Bosker, 1992
Bosker & Witziers, 1995, 1996
Brookover, Beady, Flood,
    Schweitzer, & Wisenbaker, 1979
Brookover et al., 1978
Bryk & Raudenbush, 1992
Bryk, Sebring, Allensworth,
    Luppescu, & Easton, 2010
Creemers, 1994
Eberts & Stone, 1988
Edmonds, 1979a, 1979b, 1979c,
    1981a, 1981b
Goldstein, 1997
Good & Brophy, 1986

Levine & Lezotte, 1990
Luyten, 1994
Madaus, Kellaghan, Rakow, &
    King, 1979
Mortimore, Sammons, Stoll,
    Lewis, & Ecob, 1988
Purkey & Smith, 1983
Raudenbush & Bryk, 1988
Raudenbush & Willms, 1995
Reynolds & Teddlie, 2000a,
    2000b
Rowe & Hill, 1994
Rowe, Hill, & Holmes-Smith,
    1995

Rutter, Maughan, Mortimore,
    Ouston, & Smith, 1979
Sammons, 1999
Sammons, Hillman, &
    Mortimore, 1995
Scheerens, 1992
Scheerens & Bosker, 1997
Stringfield & Teddlie, 1989
Townsend, 2007a, 2007b
van der Werf, 1997
Walberg, 1984
Wang, Haertel, & Walberg, 1993
Wright, Horn, & Sanders, 1997

To identify and describe specific factors that affect students' achievement in school, researcher John Hattie (2009, 2012) synthesized close to sixty thousand studies and found that 150 factors correlated significantly with student achievement. Although a few of these factors are outside of a school's control, the vast majority represent activities and initiatives that schools can implement and cultivate to increase their effectiveness. Hattie's top fifty factors are listed in table I.1. Those that a school *can* control are shaded.

Table I.1: Top Fifty Factors Influencing Student Achievement

Hattie (2009, 2012)

1	Self-reported grades and student expectations *SEL*	26	Comprehension programs
2	Piagetian programs *SEL*	27	Concept mapping
3	Response to intervention *SEL*	28	Cooperative versus individualistic learning *SEL*
4	Teacher credibility *SEL*	29	Direct instruction
5	Providing formative evaluation	30	Tactile stimulation programs
6	Microteaching	31	Mastery learning
7	Classroom discussion	32	Worked examples
8	Comprehensive interventions for learning-disabled students	33	Visual-perception programs
9	Teacher clarity	34	Peer tutoring *SEL*
10	Feedback	35	Cooperative versus competitive learning *SEL*
11	Reciprocal teaching	36	Phonics instruction
12	Teacher-student relationships	37	Student-centered teaching
13	Spaced versus mass practice	38	Classroom cohesion *SEL*
14	Metacognitive strategies *SEL*	39	Pre-term birth weight
15	Acceleration	40	Keller Personalized System of Instruction (PSI)
16	Classroom behavior *SEL*	41	Peer influences *SEL*
17	Vocabulary programs	42	Classroom management *SEL*
18	Repeated reading programs	43	Outdoor and adventure programs
19	Creativity programs on achievement *SEL*	44	Home environment
20	Prior achievement	45	Socioeconomic status
21	Self-verbalization and self-questioning *SEL*	46	Interactive video methods
22	Study skills	47	Professional development
23	Teaching strategies	48	Goals *SEL*
24	Problem-solving strategies *SEL*	49	Play programs *SEL*
25	Not labeling students	50	Second- and third-chance programs *SEL*

Source: Data from Hattie, 2009, 2012.

As indicated in table I.1, forty-six of the top fifty factors (92 percent) are within a school's control.

For decades, schools have used educational research like Hattie's to select individual factors to implement in their schools. For example, many schools have implemented response to intervention (RTI), the third factor in Hattie's list. Other schools have implemented formative evaluation systems, the fifth factor in Hattie's list. In some cases, schools have worked to improve their effectiveness relative to one, two, or several factors. While those efforts are laudable, they represent too narrow a focus. All of Hattie's factors need to be arranged in a hierarchy that will allow schools to focus on sets of related factors, progressively addressing and achieving increasingly more sophisticated levels of effectiveness.

From a high reliability perspective, the factors identified in the research to date are best organized into the five hierarchical levels shown in table I.2.

Table I.2: Levels of Operation for a High Reliability School

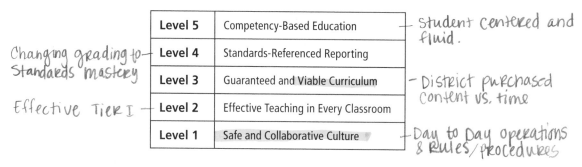

Level 5	Competency-Based Education
Level 4	Standards-Referenced Reporting
Level 3	Guaranteed and Viable Curriculum
Level 2	Effective Teaching in Every Classroom
Level 1	Safe and Collaborative Culture

Handwritten annotations:
- Changing grading to Standards' mastery
- Effective Tier I
- Student centered and fluid.
- District purchased content vs. time
- Day to Day operations & Rules/Procedures

The hierarchical relationship of the levels depicted in table I.2 has some intuitive appeal. Level 1 can be considered foundational to all other levels. If students and faculty do not have a safe and collaborative culture in which to work, little if any substantive work can be accomplished. In essence, level 1 addresses the day-to-day operation of a school: What are the rules? How do we follow them? What will happen when the rules are not followed? How do we work together to make the school run optimally?

Level 2 addresses the most commonly cited characteristic of effective schools: high-quality instruction in every classroom. Stated differently, school leaders must make sure classroom teachers are using instructional strategies in a way that reaches all students and are taking appropriate steps to improve teacher competence when this goal is not being met.

High-quality instruction is a prerequisite for level 3, a guaranteed and viable curriculum. *Guaranteed* means that the same curriculum is taught by all teachers so that all students have an equal opportunity to learn it. *Viable* means that the amount of content in the curriculum is appropriate to the amount of time teachers have available to teach it (DuFour & Marzano, 2011; Marzano, 2003b). Levels 1 through 3 are common fare among current efforts to make schools more effective.

Level 4 moves into a more rarefied level of school reform, because it involves reporting individual students' progress on specific standards. At any point in time, the leaders of a level 4 school can identify individual students' strengths and weaknesses relative to specific topics in each subject area.

Level 5 schools exist in the most rarefied group of all—one in which students move to the next level of content as soon as they demonstrate competence at the previous level. Matriculation, then, is not based on the amount of time a student spends in a given course, but rather on his or her demonstrated mastery of content.

 student centered

Leading and Lagging Indicators

In order to know what to work on and to measure their success at each level, school leaders need ways to assess their school's current status, gauge their progress through each level, and confirm successful achievement of each level. Leading and lagging indicators are useful to these ends. The distinction between leading and lagging indicators is this: leading indicators show what a school should work on to achieve a high reliability level (they provide direction), and lagging indicators are the evidence a school gives to validate its achievement of a high reliability level (they provide proof), particularly in areas where there is general agreement that the school is not doing well.

Leading indicators are "important conditions that are known to be associated with improvement" (Foley et al., n.d., p. 2). That is, they help school leaders decide what to work on to achieve high reliability status at a specific level. For example, at level 1, one leading indicator is "Faculty and staff perceive the school environment as safe and orderly." School leaders can use a survey to measure the extent to which faculty and staff perceive the school environment as safe and orderly. If perceptions of safety and orderliness are very high, school leaders may not need to focus on that area. If perceptions of safety and orderliness are low, school leaders might decide to implement initiatives or programs designed to improve the safety and orderliness of the school environment. Alternatively, low average scores on particular items might indicate that an area is not important in the school. For example, at level 1, town hall meetings and community business luncheons may or may not be important considerations for a school. Essentially, leading indicators help school leaders identify areas that are important to the school in which the school is already doing well, areas that are important to the school and need to be addressed, and areas that are not important to the school. For areas that are important to the school (both those that need to be addressed and those in which the school is already doing well), lagging indicators can be designed.

Leading Indicators via surveys

Lagging indicators provide concrete evidence that a school has achieved a specific high level of performance, particularly in an area initially flagged for low performance. For example, at level 1, a school where the faculty and staff do not perceive the school environment as safe and orderly (a leading indicator) might formulate the following lagging indicator to measure their progress toward a safe and orderly environment: "Few, if any, incidents occur in which rules and procedures are not followed." To meet this lagging indicator, school leaders would have to determine how many incidents constitute a "few." This number is called a *criterion score*; it is the score a school is aiming to achieve for the lagging indicator. School leaders then track the actual number of incidents occurring in the school and compare the number of incidents to the criterion score. If the results meet the criterion score, the school considers itself to have met that lagging indicator and the evidence can be used to validate the school's achievement of a specific high reliability level. If the results do not meet the criterion score, the school continues or adjusts its efforts until it does meet the score.

Lagging Indicators set C.S. and adjust plan

To design lagging indicators and criterion scores, school leaders can use several different approaches. The first is a percentage approach wherein school leaders create a lagging indicator that states a certain percentage of responses or data collected will meet a specific criterion. For example, a percentage lagging indicator for level 1 might be "Ninety percent of survey responses will indicate agreement that the school is safe and orderly." School leaders can use a sentence stem such as "_____ percent of responses or data will _____" to formulate percentage lagging indicators.

C.S. Lagging sentence stem

A second approach involves setting a cutoff score, below which no responses or data will fall. The following is a possible cutoff lagging indicator for level 2: "No teachers will improve less than two levels on the scale for each of their growth goals each year." School leaders could use a sentence stem such as "No responses or data will fall below _____" to compose cutoff lagging indicators.

Cutoff score stem

In cases where a school has received fairly high initial survey responses but still wants to improve, school leaders can choose to set lagging indicators for specific amounts of growth. A growth lagging indicator for level 3 might say, "Survey responses regarding all students having adequate opportunity to learn will improve 10 percent." An appropriate sentence stem for growth lagging indicators would be "Responses or data will be _____ percent higher than original responses or data."

Growth Stem

Finally, lagging indicators can be designed around the creation of a concrete product as evidence of high levels of performance. A concrete product lagging indicator for level 4 might say, "Written goals are available for each student in terms of his or her performance on common assessments." School leaders could use a sentence stem such as "A document or report stating _____ exists" to design concrete product lagging indicators.

Concrete product stem

The following chapters list leading indicators for each level. Lagging indicators, however, must be formulated for each specific school by its leaders. Schools should identify lagging indicators and set criterion scores that are appropriate to their unique situation and needs. In each chapter, we provide a template leaders can use to formulate lagging indicators and set criterion scores for each level.

Implementing Critical Commitments

After creating lagging indicators for a level, school leaders implement specific activities or initiatives that help them meet the goals inherent in the lagging indicators. For example, if a school's lagging indicator states that they will average no more than one incident per month in which rules or procedures are not followed, and they currently average five such incidents per month, they must implement activities or initiatives that change the current state of the school.

We refer to the suggested activities or initiatives that school leaders implement to meet their lagging indicators as *critical commitments.* It is important to note that these commitments are based on the cumulative experience of practitioners and researchers at Marzano Research and the research and development work of Robert J. Marzano. Therefore, the critical commitments identified in this book should be considered as strong suggestions. Certainly a school can reach high reliability status for a given level without implementing these suggestions; however, years of experience have established these activities as very useful to achieving high reliability status for a given level. Critical commitments within each level are shown in table I.3.

Table I.3: HRS Critical Commitments

Level 5	Get rid of time requirements.
	Adjust reporting systems accordingly.
Level 4	Develop proficiency scales for the essential content.
	Report status and growth on the report card using proficiency scales.
Level 3	Continually monitor the viability of the curriculum.
	Create a comprehensive vocabulary program.
	Use direct instruction in knowledge application and metacognitive skills.
Level 2	Create an evaluation system whose primary purpose is teacher development:
	• The system is comprehensive and specific.
	• The system includes a developmental scale.
	• The system acknowledges and supports growth.
Level 1	Implement the professional learning community (PLC) process.

The critical commitments for each level are described in depth in the following chapters. We believe they are essential to achieving high reliability status.

Monitoring Performance for Continuous Improvement

Once a school has met the criterion scores for a level's lagging indicators, it is considered to have achieved high reliability status for that level. However, being a high reliability school at a given level involves more than meeting criterion scores for lagging indicators. Recall from the previous discussion of high reliability organizations that implementing processes and procedures to prevent problems is only part of what they do. High reliability organizations also constantly monitor critical factors, looking for changes in data that indicate the presence of problems.

Similarly, high reliability schools monitor critical factors and immediately take action to contain and resolve the negative effects of problems as quickly as possible. Even after a school has achieved high reliability status for a specific level, its leaders continue to collect and analyze data related to leading and lagging indicators to ensure that the expectations of that level are continuously met over time. In the event that data for a specific indicator cease to meet expectations, school leaders intervene to identify the problem, minimize any negative effects of the problem, and either strengthen existing processes and procedures or implement new ones to fix the current problem and prevent future ones.

Constantly monitoring critical factors for problems requires continual data collection and observation. Consider an organization with very little tolerance for errors: the U.S. Navy. Particularly, consider an aircraft carrier, a ship from which fighter jets, helicopters, and other aircraft take off and land. The number of potential errors in such an environment is mind-boggling. For example, even small debris—like a pebble or scrap of cloth—on the flight deck can cause catastrophic problems for the finely tuned engines and other sensitive systems of naval aircraft. Therefore, the U.S. Navy implements systematic *FOD walks*. FOD stands for "foreign objects and debris," and during a FOD walk, personnel on the aircraft carrier walk along the deck shoulder to shoulder, picking up anything that they find. Such procedures occur multiple times each day. Figure I.1 shows a FOD walk being conducted on board an aircraft carrier.

Source: U.S. Navy, 2005. In public domain.

Figure I.1: FOD walk being conducted on board an aircraft carrier.

As seen here, FOD walks require all members of a ship's crew to work together to identify and resolve potential problems.

Consider another example of the power of continual data collection and monitoring. Studies show that daily weigh-ins help individuals lose weight and keep it off (for example, see Linde, Jeffery, French, Pronk,

& Boyle, 2005, and Wing, Tate, Gorin, Raynor, & Fava, 2006). Each time someone steps on the scale, that person collects a data point that shows whether he or she is moving toward or away from the target. If data show that he or she is not moving toward or maintaining the goal, he or she can take steps to minimize the impact of errors (such as eating less at meals or snacking less frequently).

In the same way that aircraft carrier crews walk along the flight deck or a dieter steps on the scale every day, so too must teachers and administrators monitor the reliability of their school even after they have achieved high reliability status at a specific level. Such work can be accomplished through quick data, problem prevention and celebration of success, and level-appropriate data collection.

Quick Data

Monitoring can be done quite efficiently through the use of *quick data*—information that can be collected quickly and easily within a short span of time. In the following chapters, we describe how schools can collect quick data about indicators for each level. Once a school has achieved high reliability status for a given level, its leaders can generate quick data on any topic, even if that topic is an area of strength for the school (as indicated by initial survey results). Quick data are meant to be used to monitor the pulse of a school regarding a particular level of performance. Therefore, a school should focus its quick data collection on indicators that will best help it monitor fluctuations in performance at a particular level of high reliability status. There are three types of quick data: (1) quick conversations, (2) quick observations, and (3) easy-to-collect quantitative data.

Quick Conversations

As the name implies, quick conversations are brief discussions that occur between teachers charged with collecting quick data and various members of a school community. For example, questions such as "How safe has our school been lately?" might be designed around leading indicators 1.1 and 1.2, which deal with safety (see chapter 1). Similarly, questions could be designed for leading indicator 1.3, which deals with teachers' having a voice in school decisions (see chapter 1), by asking, "Recently, to what extent have teachers had roles in making important decisions regarding the school?" One or more of these questions would be asked of teachers, students, and parents over a short interval of time (for example, during a specific week).

Members of collaborative teams within a PLC are perfect candidates for quick conversations. For example, consider a school that designs or selects (from the lists of questions in chapters 1 through 5) questions every month for each high reliability level it has already achieved. One or more members selected from a collaborative team are then invited to ask these questions of teachers, students, or community members (whichever groups are appropriate) and engage in five to ten quick conversations with appropriate members of the school community. These conversations last only a few minutes and occur with those school community members who are readily available. Immediately after each interaction, the teacher asking the questions codes each answer using a scale like the following:

> **Excellent**—The answer indicates that the respondent believes the school is performing above what would normally be expected for this issue.
>
> **Adequate**—The answer indicates that the respondent believes there are no major problems relative to this issue.
>
> **Unsatisfactory**—The answer indicates that the respondent believes there are major problems that should be addressed relative to this issue.

The teacher asking the questions records the responses on a form such as that in figure I.2.

Person Responding	Question	Response Code	Notes
(Teacher) Student Administrator Parent Other:	Question 1: How safe has our school been lately?	Adequate	Feels safe. Hasn't encountered any major rule infractions in the past three weeks. Recalled one minor infraction in same period.
	Question 2: To what extent have teachers had roles in making important decisions regarding the school?	Unsatisfactory	Feels unheard. Indicated that it has been months since a school leader asked for her opinion.

Figure I.2: Sample quick conversations response form.

*Visit **marzanoresearch.com/reproducibles/leadership** to download a reproducible version of this form.*

Notice that the collaborative team member who initiated the quick conversation has recorded the respondent's role (teacher), the questions asked, the code assigned to each response (adequate for question 1, unsatisfactory for question 2), and any pertinent notes from the conversation.

At the end of the month, the team aggregates the responses, as depicted in figure I.3.

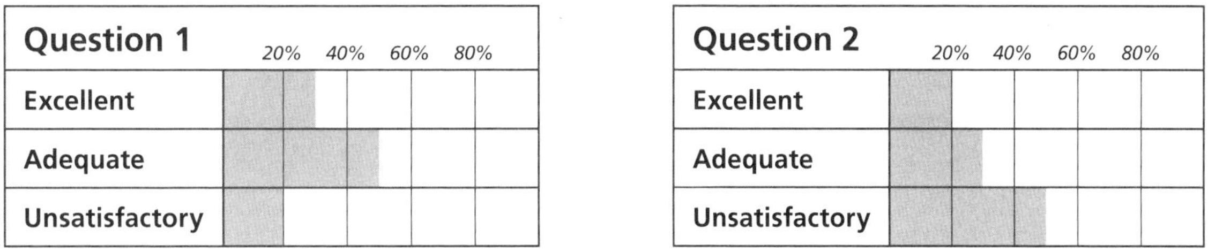

Figure I.3: Aggregated quick conversation responses.

Visual representations of data, such as those in figure I.3, allow school leaders to quickly identify problems, take steps to mitigate their effects, and resolve unsatisfactory situations. Here, school leaders might decide to reexamine the processes in place to collect information about teachers' opinions. Additionally, graphs like these give members of the school community a quick look at areas where the school is excelling and allow for celebrations of success.

Quick Observations

Like quick conversations, quick observations are made by teachers from collaborative teams. As the name implies, quick observations are specific events teachers look for. For example, for the first two leading indicators at level 1, teachers could be asked to observe recent incidents that indicate the following:

- The school is a safe place.
- The school is an unsafe place.
- The school is an orderly place.
- The school is not an orderly place.

School leaders could also design observation prompts from their school's lagging indicators. Quick observation data would be collected anecdotally. Table I.4 shows one collaborative team member's anecdotal notes about incidents observed over the course of a week.

Table I.4: Anecdotal Notes for Quick Observations

	Recent incidents that indicate the school is a safe place	Recent incidents that indicate the school is an unsafe place	Recent incidents that indicate the school is an orderly place	Recent incidents that indicate the school is not an orderly place
Monday	Student turned in $20 found in hallway		Students reacted according to safety plan when fire alarm went off	Fumes from science lab set off fire alarm
Tuesday	Student club members created posters for school hallways encouraging kindness and compassion			Shreds of paper and glitter left in hallway after students worked on a project there
Wednesday	Administrators present in all main hallways during passing periods	Two students shouting at each other after school while waiting for busses; teachers helped resolve	Checked out a cart of tablets; tablets were cleaned after last use and neatly arranged; no accessories missing	
Thursday	Students made comments on social media sites about how much they enjoy specific classes		Cafeteria very clean after lunch period; all trash thrown away and tables cleared	
Friday		Slippery floors this morning because of rain; almost fell	Students picked up trash blown onto athletic field by storm	

Visit **marzanoresearch.com/reproducibles/leadership** *to download a reproducible version of this form.*

On a regular basis, notes (such as those in table I.4) collected by collaborative team members could be compiled into a narrative summary and shared with members of the school community.

Easy-to-Collect Quantitative Data

In many schools, easy-to-collect quantitative data are available and can be used to monitor progress on a regular basis. Such data are typically collected by school leaders. For example, if a school leader already has in place a system that keeps track of student absences and tardies, she would aggregate these data once a month as a way of monitoring level 1 performance.

Problem Prevention and Celebration of Success

As schools achieve higher levels of reliability, they should continue to monitor each level already achieved. Thus, a school that has achieved level 3 high reliability status will constantly monitor data for levels 1, 2, and 3 as it works on level 4. If quick data show that performance is unsatisfactory at any level, schools take steps to remedy the situation. In this way, problems are resolved before they cause significant errors in the system.

Problem prevention is an excellent reason to constantly monitor critical factors and address errors immediately. However, it is not the only reason to monitor performance. Tracking performance using quick data allows school leaders to celebrate successes with staff members, parents, and students. Research by Edwin Locke and Gary Latham (2002) has shown that feedback—especially positive feedback—is important in keeping people motivated to achieve or maintain goals:

> For goals to be effective, people need summary feedback that reveals progress in relation to their goals. If they do not know how they are doing, it is difficult or impossible for them to adjust the level or direction of their effort or to adjust their performance strategies to match what the goal requires. . . . When people find they are below target, they normally increase their effort . . . or try a new strategy. . . . After people attain the goal they have been pursuing, they generally set a higher goal for themselves. (p. 708)

School leaders can use quick data to regularly celebrate the school's successes; congratulate students, teachers, and parents on their hard work; and motivate the school community toward continuous improvement.

Level-Appropriate Data Collection

As mentioned previously, schools should not only collect quick data for the level they are currently working to achieve but also for all of the lower levels they have already attained. However, we do not advise that schools try to collect data for levels higher than the one they are currently working on, because data for higher levels often *cannot* be collected by schools at lower levels. This is particularly true for levels 4 and 5. For example, a visitor to a school working on level 5 (that is, a school that has already achieved high reliability status at levels 1, 2, 3, and 4) might ask a student, "What level are you at in mathematics? Science? Social studies? English language arts? What measurement topics are you working on? What is your current score on those measurement topics? What are you doing to raise your score?" The student should be able to answer most, if not all, of these questions. However, a visitor who asked a student in a school working on level 2 the same questions would likely get a blank look. Because the school is not working on level 5, it is impossible to collect level 5 data there.

The hierarchical nature of our model is one of its most powerful aspects. Each level guarantees that a school is also performing at all of the lower levels. So, if a school is working on level 4 and has achieved levels 1, 2, and 3, it is guaranteed that the school has a safe and collaborative culture, effective teaching in every classroom, and a guaranteed and viable curriculum. By definition, working on level 4 means that lagging indicators for the first three levels have been met and the status of each is continually monitored. Each level supports the one above it and guarantees specific outcomes for those below it.

Overview of the Model

The process of achieving high reliability status for a given level is fairly straightforward. The teacher and administrator leading indicator surveys (from chapters 1 through 5) are administered, and if a school wants a more comprehensive set of data, the student and parent surveys are also administered. Scores on the surveys are analyzed to determine the school's strengths and weaknesses. The analysis process for interpreting survey results should be designed to identify those items that represent actions considered important to the effective functioning of the school and whose average scores are low.

Items that have these characteristics are candidates for interventions—programs or practices the school will implement to shore up weak areas. Once these programs or practices are in full implementation, a school identifies one or more lagging indicators that either have explicit criterion scores or are concrete enough to be clear about whether their requirements have been satisfied. Once the requirements for satisfying the lagging indicators have been met for a given level, a school considers itself to have reached high reliability status for that level. However, the school is not finished once criterion scores have been met for a given level. Rather, the school then identifies ways to collect quick data to monitor its status and acknowledge success on a periodic basis—say, once a month.

If after administering leading indicator surveys, a school has no low scores on items that are important to the school, then it moves directly to identifying lagging indicators. Once the lagging indicators have been met, the school can consider itself to have reached high reliability status for the level and move to monitoring its status and celebrating success using quick data on a regular basis. Figure I.4 explains how to obtain high reliability status at any given level.

A school will continue the process described in figure I.4 until it has reached high reliability status at all five levels and can declare itself a high reliability school. At such a point, the school would continue to use quick data to monitor its status and success at all five levels. Whenever quick data indicate that a lagging indicator for any level has slipped below the acceptable level, the school leader immediately intervenes to bring the school up to acceptable levels of performance on the fluctuating indicator.

How to Use This Book

This handbook has one chapter for each high reliability level. Each of these chapters begins with the recommended leading indicators for that level. We then present a series of surveys (for teachers and staff, administrators, students, and parents) based on those leading indicators. School leaders can use these surveys to get a preliminary idea of what leading indicators they may need to work on. Once members of the school community have completed the surveys and the results have been compiled, school leaders can identify which, if any, leading indicators need to be addressed in the school.

To address leading indicators, school leaders can use the critical commitments detailed in the chapter for each level: chapter 1 addresses how to implement the professional learning community (PLC) process; chapter 2 gives guidance about creating an evaluation system whose primary purpose is teacher development; chapter 3 speaks to continually monitoring the viability of the curriculum, creating a comprehensive vocabulary program, and using direct instruction in knowledge application and metacognitive skills; chapter 4 focuses on developing proficiency scales for essential content and reporting status and growth on the report card using those proficiency scales; and chapter 5 gives direction about getting rid of time requirements and adjusting reporting systems accordingly. These critical commitments can guide leaders as they work on areas identified by the leading indicator surveys.

If survey results indicate that no leading indicators need to be addressed, school leaders can move on to identifying lagging indicators and criterion scores that will be used to measure whether or not the school has achieved high reliability status for the level. To facilitate this process, each chapter provides a template that leaders can use to identify these indicators and scores, as well as example lagging indicators that school leaders could use. Once the lagging indicators have been created and the criterion scores set, school leaders gather data and other information to track their progress toward and achievement of high reliability status for that level.

Finally, each chapter lists specific questions (for quick conversations) and incidents (for quick observations) that school leaders can use to gather quick data for that level. Each chapter also provides examples of easy-to-collect quantitative data, which allow school leaders to continually monitor their school's performance on previously achieved high reliability levels and celebrate success.

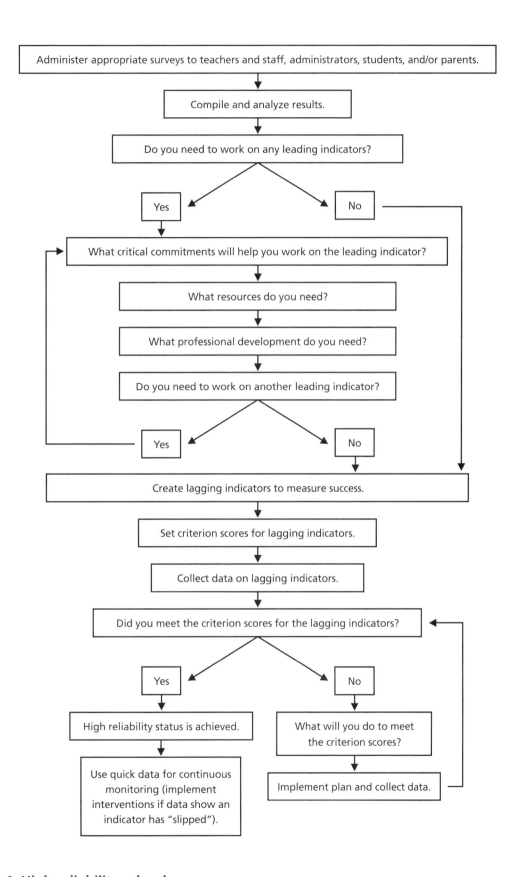

Figure I.4: High reliability schools process.

Chapter 1
Safe and Collaborative Culture

● ● ●

Level 1 addresses the factors considered foundational to the well-being of a school. Namely, do faculty, staff, students, parents, and the community feel that the school is safe and maximizes collaboration for the enhancement of student learning? Level 1 has eight leading indicators:

1.1   The faculty and staff perceive the school environment as safe and orderly.

1.2   Students, parents, and the community perceive the school environment as safe and orderly.

1.3   Teachers have formal roles in the decision-making process regarding school initiatives.

1.4   Teacher teams and collaborative groups regularly interact to address common issues regarding curriculum, assessment, instruction, and the achievement of all students.

1.5   Teachers and staff have formal ways to provide input regarding the optimal functioning of the school.

1.6   Students, parents, and the community have formal ways to provide input regarding the optimal functioning of the school.

1.7   The success of the whole school, as well as individuals within the school, is appropriately acknowledged.

1.8   The fiscal, operational, and technological resources of the school are managed in a way that directly supports teachers.

As explained in the introduction, the leading indicators are designed to help school leaders determine what is already working well in their school and identify areas in need of focused attention. One of the best ways to accomplish this is to administer a leading indicator survey to teachers and staff, administrators, students, and parents.

Level 1 Short-Form Leading Indicator Survey

Figure 1.1 (page 16) presents a short-form leading indicator survey for level 1. This survey can be administered to faculty, staff, and administrators within a school. Visit **marzanoresearch.com/hrs** for a reproducible version of the short-form survey items for all five levels.

| 1: Strongly disagree | 2: Disagree | 3: Neither disagree nor agree |
| 4: Agree | 5: Strongly agree | N: N/A or don't know |

	1	2	3	4	5	N
1.1 The faculty and staff perceive the school environment as safe and orderly.	1	2	3	4	5	N
1.2 Students, parents, and the community perceive the school environment as safe and orderly.	1	2	3	4	5	N
1.3 Teachers have formal roles in the decision-making process regarding school initiatives.	1	2	3	4	5	N
1.4 Teacher teams and collaborative groups regularly interact to address common issues regarding curriculum, assessment, instruction, and the achievement of all students.	1	2	3	4	5	N
1.5 Teachers and staff have formal ways to provide input regarding the optimal functioning of the school.	1	2	3	4	5	N
1.6 Students, parents, and the community have formal ways to provide input regarding the optimal functioning of the school.	1	2	3	4	5	N
1.7 The success of the whole school, as well as individuals within the school, is appropriately acknowledged.	1	2	3	4	5	N
1.8 The fiscal, operational, and technological resources of the school are managed in a way that directly supports teachers.	1	2	3	4	5	N

Figure 1.1: Level 1 short-form leading indicator survey.

This survey provides very general information about a school's level 1 status. For more specific information, long-form surveys should be used.

Level 1 Long-Form Leading Indicator Surveys

Here, we present long-form surveys for four different audiences: (1) teachers and staff, (2) administrators, (3) students, and (4) parents. These surveys provide detailed information for each leading indicator. School leaders ask teachers and staff members, administrators, students, and parents to complete the appropriate survey from reproducibles 1.1–1.4 (pages 17–26). Leaders then examine the results to identify areas of perceived strength or weakness within the school. It is important to note that a school can and should adapt these surveys. School leaders can delete items not relevant to their particular school. They can also add or change items to meet the specific needs of their school.

Reproducible 1.1: Level 1 Long-Form Leading Indicator Survey for Teachers and Staff

| 1: Strongly disagree | 2: Disagree | 3: Neither disagree nor agree |
| 4: Agree | 5: Strongly agree | N: N/A or don't know |

		1	2	3	4	5	N
1.1 The faculty and staff perceive the school environment as safe and orderly.	Our school is a safe place.	1	2	3	4	5	N
	Our school is an orderly place.	1	2	3	4	5	N
	Our school has clear and specific rules and procedures in place.	1	2	3	4	5	N
	I know the emergency management procedures for our school.	1	2	3	4	5	N
	I know how to implement the emergency management procedures for our school.	1	2	3	4	5	N
	My students and I regularly practice implementing emergency management procedures for specific incidents.	1	2	3	4	5	N
	Our school's emergency management procedures are updated on a regular basis.	1	2	3	4	5	N
1.2 Students, parents, and the community perceive the school environment as safe and orderly.	Students and their parents describe our school as a safe place.	1	2	3	4	5	N
	Students and their parents describe our school as an orderly place.	1	2	3	4	5	N
	Students and their parents are aware of the rules and procedures in place at our school.	1	2	3	4	5	N
	Our school uses social media to allow anonymous reporting of potential incidents.	1	2	3	4	5	N
	Our school has a system that allows school leaders to communicate with parents about issues regarding school safety (for example, a school call-out system).	1	2	3	4	5	N
	School leaders coordinate with local law enforcement agencies regarding school safety issues.	1	2	3	4	5	N
	School leaders engage parents and the community regarding school safety issues.	1	2	3	4	5	N
1.3 Teachers have formal roles in the decision-making process regarding school initiatives.	It is clear which types of decisions will be made with direct teacher input.	1	2	3	4	5	N
	Techniques and systems are in place to collect data and information from teachers on a regular basis.	1	2	3	4	5	N
	Notes and reports exist documenting how teacher input was used to make specific decisions.	1	2	3	4	5	N
	Electronic tools (for example, online survey tools) are used to collect teachers' opinions regarding specific decisions.	1	2	3	4	5	N
	Groups of teachers are targeted to provide input regarding specific decisions.	1	2	3	4	5	N

1.4 Teacher teams and collaborative groups regularly interact to address common issues regarding curriculum, assessment, instruction, and the achievement of all students.	A professional learning community (PLC) process is in place in our school.	1	2	3	4	5	N
	Our school's PLC collaborative teams have written goals.	1	2	3	4	5	N
	School leaders regularly examine PLC collaborative teams' progress toward their goals.	1	2	3	4	5	N
	Our school's PLC collaborative teams create common assessments.	1	2	3	4	5	N
	Our school's PLC collaborative teams analyze student achievement and growth.	1	2	3	4	5	N
	Data teams are in place in our school.	1	2	3	4	5	N
	Our school's data teams have written goals.	1	2	3	4	5	N
	School leaders regularly examine data teams' progress toward their goals.	1	2	3	4	5	N
	School leaders collect and review minutes and notes from PLC collaborative team and data team meetings to ensure that teams are focusing on student achievement.	1	2	3	4	5	N
1.5 Teachers and staff have formal ways to provide input regarding the optimal functioning of the school.	Data collection systems are in place to collect opinion data from teachers and staff regarding the optimal functioning of our school.	1	2	3	4	5	N
	Opinion data collected from teachers and staff are archived.	1	2	3	4	5	N
	Reports of opinion data from teachers and staff are regularly generated.	1	2	3	4	5	N
	The manner in which opinion data from teachers and staff are used is transparent.	1	2	3	4	5	N
	Our school improvement team regularly provides input and feedback about our school's improvement plan.	1	2	3	4	5	N
1.6 Students, parents, and the community have formal ways to provide input regarding the optimal functioning of the school.	Data collection systems are in place to collect opinion data from students, parents, and the community regarding the optimal functioning of our school.	1	2	3	4	5	N
	Opinion data collected from students, parents, and the community are archived.	1	2	3	4	5	N
	Reports of opinion data from students, parents, and the community are regularly generated.	1	2	3	4	5	N
	The manner in which opinion data from students, parents, and the community are used is transparent.	1	2	3	4	5	N
	Our school hosts an interactive website for students, parents, and the community.	1	2	3	4	5	N
	I use social networking technologies (such as Twitter and Facebook) to involve students, parents, and the community.	1	2	3	4	5	N
	School leaders host virtual town hall meetings.	1	2	3	4	5	N
	School leaders conduct focus group meetings with students, parents, and the community.	1	2	3	4	5	N
	School leaders host or speak at community/business luncheons.	1	2	3	4	5	N

1.7 The success of the whole school, as well as individuals within the school, is appropriately acknowledged.	Our school's accomplishments have been adequately acknowledged and celebrated.	1	2	3	4	5	N
	My team's or department's accomplishments have been adequately acknowledged and celebrated.	1	2	3	4	5	N
	My individual accomplishments have been adequately acknowledged and celebrated.	1	2	3	4	5	N
	School leaders acknowledge and celebrate individual accomplishments, teacher-team or department accomplishments, and whole-school accomplishments in a variety of ways (for example, through faculty celebrations, newsletters to parents, announcements, the school website, or social media).	1	2	3	4	5	N
	School leaders regularly celebrate the successes of individuals in a variety of positions in the school (such as teachers or support staff).	1	2	3	4	5	N
1.8 The fiscal, operational, and technological resources of the school are managed in a way that directly supports teachers.	I have adequate materials to teach effectively.	1	2	3	4	5	N
	I have adequate time to teach effectively.	1	2	3	4	5	N
	School leaders develop, submit, and implement detailed budgets.	1	2	3	4	5	N
	School leaders successfully access and leverage a variety of fiscal resources (such as grants or title funds).	1	2	3	4	5	N
	School leaders manage time to maximize a focus on instruction.	1	2	3	4	5	N
	School leaders direct the use of technology to improve teaching and learning.	1	2	3	4	5	N
	School leaders provide adequate training for the instructional technology teachers are expected to use.	1	2	3	4	5	N

A Handbook for High Reliability Schools © 2014 Marzano Research • marzanoresearch.com

Reproducible 1.2: Level 1 Long-Form Leading Indicator Survey for Administrators

1: Strongly disagree	2: Disagree	3: Neither disagree nor agree
4: Agree	5: Strongly agree	N: N/A or don't know

1.1 The faculty and staff perceive the school environment as safe and orderly.	Our school is a safe place.	1	2	3	4	5	N
	Our school is an orderly place.	1	2	3	4	5	N
	Our school has clear and specific rules and procedures in place.	1	2	3	4	5	N
	Teachers and staff know the emergency management procedures for our school.	1	2	3	4	5	N
	Teachers and staff know how to implement the emergency management procedures for our school.	1	2	3	4	5	N
	Teachers, staff, and students regularly practice implementing emergency management procedures for specific incidents.	1	2	3	4	5	N
	Our school's emergency management procedures are updated on a regular basis.	1	2	3	4	5	N
1.2 Students, parents, and the community perceive the school environment as safe and orderly.	Students and their parents describe our school as a safe place.	1	2	3	4	5	N
	Students and their parents describe our school as an orderly place.	1	2	3	4	5	N
	Students and their parents are aware of the rules and procedures in place at our school.	1	2	3	4	5	N
	Our school uses social media to allow anonymous reporting of potential incidents.	1	2	3	4	5	N
	Our school has a system that allows me to communicate with parents about issues regarding school safety (for example, a school call-out system).	1	2	3	4	5	N
	I coordinate with local law enforcement agencies regarding school safety issues.	1	2	3	4	5	N
	I engage parents and the community regarding school safety issues.	1	2	3	4	5	N
1.3 Teachers have formal roles in the decision-making process regarding school initiatives.	It is clear which types of decisions will be made with direct teacher input.	1	2	3	4	5	N
	Techniques and systems are in place to collect data and information from teachers on a regular basis.	1	2	3	4	5	N
	Notes and reports exist documenting how teacher input was used to make specific decisions.	1	2	3	4	5	N
	Electronic tools (for example, online survey tools) are used to collect teachers' opinions regarding specific decisions.	1	2	3	4	5	N
	Groups of teachers are targeted to provide input regarding specific decisions.	1	2	3	4	5	N

1.4 Teacher teams and collaborative groups regularly interact to address common issues regarding curriculum, assessment, instruction, and the achievement of all students.	A professional learning community (PLC) process is in place in our school.	1	2	3	4	5	N
	Our school's PLC collaborative teams have written goals.	1	2	3	4	5	N
	I regularly examine PLC collaborative teams' progress toward their goals.	1	2	3	4	5	N
	Our school's PLC collaborative teams create common assessments.	1	2	3	4	5	N
	Our school's PLC collaborative teams analyze student achievement and growth.	1	2	3	4	5	N
	Data teams are in place in our school.	1	2	3	4	5	N
	Our school's data teams have written goals.	1	2	3	4	5	N
	I regularly examine data teams' progress toward their goals.	1	2	3	4	5	N
	I collect and review minutes and notes from PLC collaborative team and data team meetings to ensure that teams are focusing on student achievement.	1	2	3	4	5	N
1.5 Teachers and staff have formal ways to provide input regarding the optimal functioning of the school.	Data collection systems are in place to collect opinion data from teachers and staff regarding the optimal functioning of our school.	1	2	3	4	5	N
	Opinion data collected from teachers and staff are archived.	1	2	3	4	5	N
	Reports of opinion data from teachers and staff are regularly generated.	1	2	3	4	5	N
	The manner in which opinion data from teachers and staff are used is transparent.	1	2	3	4	5	N
	Our school improvement team regularly provides input and feedback about our school's improvement plan.	1	2	3	4	5	N
1.6 Students, parents, and the community have formal ways to provide input regarding the optimal functioning of the school.	Data collection systems are in place to collect opinion data from students, parents, and the community regarding the optimal functioning of our school.	1	2	3	4	5	N
	Opinion data collected from students, parents, and the community are archived.	1	2	3	4	5	N
	Reports of opinion data from students, parents, and the community are regularly generated.	1	2	3	4	5	N
	The manner in which opinion data from students, parents, and the community are used is transparent.	1	2	3	4	5	N
	Our school hosts an interactive website for students, parents, and the community.	1	2	3	4	5	N
	I use social networking technologies (such as Twitter and Facebook) to involve students, parents, and the community.	1	2	3	4	5	N
	I host virtual town hall meetings.	1	2	3	4	5	N
	I conduct focus group meetings with students, parents, and the community.	1	2	3	4	5	N
	I host or speak at community/business luncheons.	1	2	3	4	5	N

1.7 The success of the whole school, as well as individuals within the school, is appropriately acknowledged.	Our school's accomplishments have been adequately acknowledged and celebrated.	1	2	3	4	5	N
	Teacher teams' or departments' accomplishments have been adequately acknowledged and celebrated.	1	2	3	4	5	N
	Individual teachers' accomplishments have been adequately acknowledged and celebrated.	1	2	3	4	5	N
	I acknowledge and celebrate individual accomplishments, teacher-team or department accomplishments, and whole-school accomplishments in a variety of ways (for example, through faculty celebrations, newsletters to parents, announcements, the school website, or social media).	1	2	3	4	5	N
	I regularly celebrate the successes of individuals in a variety of positions in the school (such as teachers or support staff).	1	2	3	4	5	N
1.8 The fiscal, operational, and technological resources of the school are managed in a way that directly supports teachers.	Teachers have adequate materials to teach effectively.	1	2	3	4	5	N
	Teachers have adequate time to teach effectively.	1	2	3	4	5	N
	I develop, submit, and implement detailed budgets.	1	2	3	4	5	N
	I successfully access and leverage a variety of fiscal resources (such as grants or title funds).	1	2	3	4	5	N
	I manage time to maximize a focus on instruction.	1	2	3	4	5	N
	I direct the use of technology to improve teaching and learning.	1	2	3	4	5	N
	I provide adequate training for the instructional technology teachers are expected to use.	1	2	3	4	5	N

A Handbook for High Reliability Schools © 2014 Marzano Research • marzanoresearch.com

Reproducible 1.3: Level 1 Long-Form Leading Indicator Survey for Students

1: Strongly disagree	2: Disagree	3: Neither disagree nor agree
4: Agree	5: Strongly agree	N: N/A or don't know

1.1 The faculty and staff perceive the school environment as safe and orderly.	I know what to do if an emergency happens at school (such as a tornado, fire, lockdown, or medical emergency).	1	2	3	4	5	N
1.2 Students, parents, and the community perceive the school environment as safe and orderly.	My school is a safe place.	1	2	3	4	5	N
	My school is an orderly place.	1	2	3	4	5	N
	I know the rules and procedures at my school.	1	2	3	4	5	N
	I can use social media to report bullying or other incidents anonymously.	1	2	3	4	5	N
1.3 Teachers have formal roles in the decision-making process regarding school initiatives.	Teachers help make important decisions at my school.	1	2	3	4	5	N
1.4 Teacher teams and collaborative groups regularly interact to address common issues regarding curriculum, assessment, instruction, and the achievement of all students.	My teachers meet together on a regular basis.	1	2	3	4	5	N
1.5 Teachers and staff have formal ways to provide input regarding the optimal functioning of the school.	My school's leaders collect information from teachers about their opinions.	1	2	3	4	5	N
1.6 Students, parents, and the community have formal ways to provide input regarding the optimal functioning of the school.	My school's leaders ask for my opinion about how the school should function.	1	2	3	4	5	N
1.7 The success of the whole school, as well as individuals within the school, is appropriately acknowledged.	When I achieve a goal or accomplish something important, my school's leaders, my teachers, and other students celebrate it.	1	2	3	4	5	N
1.8 The fiscal, operational, and technological resources of the school are managed in a way that directly supports teachers.	I have plenty of time to learn.	1	2	3	4	5	N
	Teachers in my school use technology to help me learn.	1	2	3	4	5	N

Reproducible 1.4: Level 1 Long-Form Leading Indicator Survey for Parents

| 1: Strongly disagree | 2: Disagree | 3: Neither disagree nor agree |
| 4: Agree | 5: Strongly agree | N: N/A or don't know |

1.1 The faculty and staff perceive the school environment as safe and orderly.	Teachers and staff at my child's school consider it a safe place.	1	2	3	4	5	N
	Teachers and staff at my child's school consider it an orderly place.	1	2	3	4	5	N
	My child's school has clear and specific rules and procedures in place.	1	2	3	4	5	N
	Teachers, staff, and my child know the emergency management procedures for the school.	1	2	3	4	5	N
	Teachers, staff, and my child know how to implement the emergency management procedures for the school.	1	2	3	4	5	N
	Teachers, staff, and my child have practiced implementing emergency management procedures for specific incidents (for example, tornado drills, fire drills, or lockdown drills).	1	2	3	4	5	N
	The emergency management procedures at my child's school are updated on a regular basis.	1	2	3	4	5	N
1.2 Students, parents, and the community perceive the school environment as safe and orderly.	My child's school is a safe place.	1	2	3	4	5	N
	My child's school is an orderly place.	1	2	3	4	5	N
	I am aware of the rules and procedures in place at my child's school.	1	2	3	4	5	N
	My child's school uses social media to allow anonymous reporting of potential incidents.	1	2	3	4	5	N
	My child's school has a system that allows school leaders to communicate with me about issues regarding school safety (for example, a school call-out system).	1	2	3	4	5	N
	The leaders of my child's school coordinate with local law enforcement agencies regarding school safety issues.	1	2	3	4	5	N
	The leaders of my child's school engage the community and me regarding school safety issues.	1	2	3	4	5	N
1.3 Teachers have formal roles in the decision-making process regarding school initiatives.	Teachers help make important decisions at my child's school.	1	2	3	4	5	N
	Specific groups of teachers provide input regarding specific decisions at my child's school.	1	2	3	4	5	N

page 1 of 3

1.4 Teacher teams and collaborative groups regularly interact to address common issues regarding curriculum, assessment, instruction, and the achievement of all students.	Teachers at my child's school meet together on a regular basis.	1	2	3	4	5	N
	At my child's school, teachers who teach the same subject use the same exams, quizzes, and tests.	1	2	3	4	5	N
	Teams of teachers at my child's school look at student achievement data to figure out how to improve students' learning.	1	2	3	4	5	N
1.5 Teachers and staff have formal ways to provide input regarding the optimal functioning of the school.	The leaders of my child's school ask teachers for their opinions about how the school should function.	1	2	3	4	5	N
	The leaders of my child's school collect information from teachers about their opinions.	1	2	3	4	5	N
1.6 Students, parents, and the community have formal ways to provide input regarding the optimal functioning of the school.	The leaders of my child's school ask for my opinion about how the school should function.	1	2	3	4	5	N
	The leaders of my child's school have a system to save and keep track of the information they collect about my opinions.	1	2	3	4	5	N
	Reports of opinion data collected from students, parents, and the community are generated regularly.	1	2	3	4	5	N
	I understand how my opinions affect school decisions.	1	2	3	4	5	N
	My child's school hosts an interactive website.	1	2	3	4	5	N
	I visit my child's school's website often.	1	2	3	4	5	N
	The leaders and teachers at my child's school use social networking technologies (such as Twitter and Facebook) to involve students, parents, and the community.	1	2	3	4	5	N
	The leaders of my child's school host virtual town hall meetings.	1	2	3	4	5	N
	The leaders of my child's school conduct focus group meetings with students, parents, and the community.	1	2	3	4	5	N
	The leaders of my child's school host or speak at community/business luncheons.	1	2	3	4	5	N

A Handbook for High Reliability Schools © 2014 Marzano Research • marzanoresearch.com

1.7 The success of the whole school, as well as individuals within the school, is appropriately acknowledged.	The accomplishments of my child's school have been adequately acknowledged and celebrated.	1	2	3	4	5	N
	The accomplishments of my child's teachers have been adequately acknowledged and celebrated.	1	2	3	4	5	N
	My child's individual accomplishments have been adequately acknowledged and celebrated.	1	2	3	4	5	N
	The leaders of my child's school acknowledge and celebrate individual accomplishments, teacher-team or department accomplishments, and whole-school accomplishments in a variety of ways (for example, through faculty celebrations, newsletters to parents, announcements, the school website, or social media).	1	2	3	4	5	N
1.8 The fiscal, operational, and technological resources of the school are managed in a way that directly supports teachers.	Teachers at my child's school have adequate materials to teach effectively.	1	2	3	4	5	N
	Teachers at my child's school have adequate time to teach effectively.	1	2	3	4	5	N
	The leaders of my child's school develop, submit, and implement detailed budgets.	1	2	3	4	5	N
	The leaders of my child's school successfully access and leverage a variety of fiscal resources (such as grants or title funds).	1	2	3	4	5	N
	The leaders of my child's school manage time to maximize a focus on instruction.	1	2	3	4	5	N
	The leaders of my child's school direct the use of technology to improve teaching and learning.	1	2	3	4	5	N

A Handbook for High Reliability Schools © 2014 Marzano Research • marzanoresearch.com

After administering the survey and compiling the results, school leaders might notice that faculty and staff responses to leading indicator 1.4, which is "Teacher teams and collaborative groups regularly interact to address common issues regarding curriculum, assessment, instruction, and the achievement of all students," are lower than responses to other leading indicators. This could prompt school leaders to implement activities and initiatives specifically designed to enhance the effectiveness of collaborative groups addressing common issues regarding curriculum, assessment, instruction, and the achievement of students. As described in the introduction, we consider implementing professional learning communities as critical to high reliability status at level 1. Hence we refer to the implementation of the PLC process as a critical commitment.

Level 1 Critical Commitment

While the PLC process is sometimes thought of as a singular intervention to engage teachers in meaningful collaboration, when used to its full potential it can be the structure that makes possible the successful implementation of a variety of the leading indicators for level 1. Indeed, Richard DuFour and Robert Marzano (2011) maintained that the PLC process can change the basic dynamic of leadership within a school, allowing school leaders to have a more efficient and direct impact on what occurs in classrooms. DuFour and Marzano noted that

> the principal of a K–5 building can now work closely with six teams rather than thirty individuals. The principal of a large high school can influence twenty team leaders directly rather than 150 teachers indirectly. In short, the PLC process provides a vehicle for focused interactions between principals and teachers. (p. 51)

DuFour and Marzano explained that in the absence of the PLC process, the principal must influence each individual teacher, who in turn influences student achievement in his or her classroom (see figure 1.2). This has long been recognized in the research literature: the principal has an indirect influence on student achievement (see Marzano, Waters, & McNulty, 2005). In figure 1.2, this indirect influence is indicated by the multiple arrows between principal actions and teacher actions.

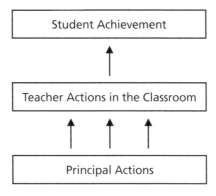

Source: DuFour & Marzano, 2011, p. 49.

Figure 1.2: Typical relationship between principal behavior and student achievement.

DuFour and Marzano (2011) further noted that one of the more enlightening and disturbing aspects of the figure is that

> multiple lines of influence are depicted between the principal and teachers' actions. This is because traditionally there has been no way for principals to interact directly and concretely with teachers in a manner that influences their actions in the classroom. (p. 49)

The PLC process alters this basic dynamic. Within the context of the collaborative team structure of a PLC, the relationship between principal behavior and student achievement can be depicted as shown in figure 1.3.

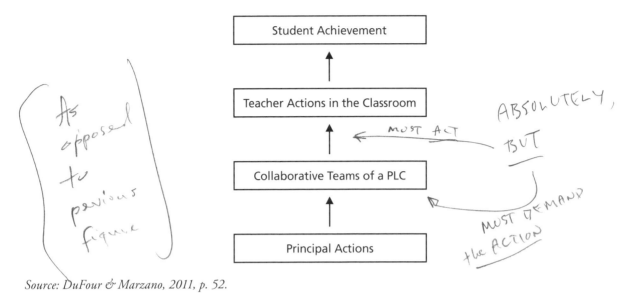

Source: DuFour & Marzano, 2011, p. 52.

Figure 1.3: Relationship between principal behavior and student achievement with PLCs.

In a PLC, principals have a direct line of influence to collaborative teams, and collaborative teams have a direct line of influence to teacher actions in the classroom (as indicated by the single arrows). In effect, use of the PLC process can render leadership more efficient.

Because of the collaborative nature of PLCs, schools can use the process to meet multiple leading indicators. The PLC process creates a foundation for leading indicators 1.1, 1.3, and 1.5 because collaborative teams can be used to identify and execute ways to make the school more safe and orderly, obtain teacher input into decisions regarding school policies, and provide input regarding how the school can function more effectively. Leading indicators 1.2 and 1.6 relate to parents and the community. It is important that initiatives and activities be designed and executed specifically for those constituent groups, and collaborative teams can aid in the design of those initiatives and activities. When done with integrity, the PLC process can also be a powerful vehicle for leading indicator 1.7, because collaborative groups can be used to identify and recognize individuals whose students have made exceptional gains in their learning. Specific collaborative teams can also be singled out and acknowledged, in addition to recognizing the entire school community for certain accomplishments. Finally, leading indicator 1.8 can also be addressed through a PLC, as collaborative teams can be used to gather information from teachers about the use of fiscal, operational, and technological resources.

Level 1 Lagging Indicators

As explained in the introduction, lagging indicators and their corresponding criterion scores provide evidence that a school has achieved a specific level of high reliability. High scores on leading indicator surveys can provide enough evidence for leaders to conclude that no immediate action is required regarding a specific area. However, low scores on leading indicators point to areas that may need to be addressed in a school. As activities and initiatives are implemented to address those areas, the school's progress should be tracked using lagging indicators. For example, if a school leader noticed very low survey scores on leading indicator 1.4, he or she might formulate a lagging indicator to measure the school's progress in that area. Lagging indicators might also be formulated for areas with high scores. Again, lagging indicators are the evidence a school gives to validate its achievement of a high reliability level, particularly in areas where there is general agreement that the school is not doing well.

To illustrate, the following are examples of lagging indicators that a school could use to demonstrate that they are meeting level 1 status:

- One or no incidents occur each year in which students' safety is compromised.
- Fewer than five incidents occur each month in which rules and procedures are not followed.
- Surveys of faculty and staff indicate 90 percent agreement that the school is safe and orderly.
- Surveys of students, parents, and the community indicate 90 percent agreement that the school is safe and orderly.
- Surveys of faculty and staff indicate 90 percent agreement that they have input regarding the optimal functioning of the school.
- Surveys of students, parents, and the community indicate 90 percent agreement that they have input regarding the optimal functioning of the school.
- Meeting minutes show that 80 percent of decisions affecting the entire school were made with input from faculty and staff.
- Meeting minutes show that 80 percent of decisions affecting the entire school were made with input from students, parents, and the community.
- Project notes indicate that 85 percent of school projects were developed through collaborative efforts of teacher teams.
- A written report is available indicating that 80 percent of the school budget is focused on issues that directly support teaching and learning.
- A written report demonstrates that specific accomplishments of the school and individuals within the school have been formally acknowledged.
- One or no incidents occur each year that indicate teacher dissatisfaction with the school (for example, teacher requests for transfers to other schools).

It is important to note that the lagging indicators listed in each chapter are only examples. There is no set number of lagging indicators a school should use, and there is no set list of lagging indicators from which a school must select. Rather, school leaders should use data from the leading indicator surveys to identify areas of importance to their school for which lagging indicators should be designed. A chart like the one in table 1.1 (page 30) can facilitate the process of moving from leading indicators to lagging indicators.

Here, we offer several examples of how schools identified areas of concern, designed lagging indicators and criterion scores or concrete products to measure their progress, and implemented plans to meet the lagging indicators.

Example 1

An elementary principal reviewing survey data for level 1 finds that although teachers, parents, and students agreed that leading indicators 1.3 through 1.8 were present in the school, they did not feel that it was safe and orderly. The low scores on leading indicators 1.1, "The faculty and staff perceive the school environment as safe and orderly," and 1.2, "Students, parents, and the community perceive the school environment as safe and orderly," prompt the principal to investigate further. He discovers that low ratings for those leading indicators are primarily due to the excessive number of physical injuries occurring on the playground.

Table 1.1: Lagging Indicator Determination Chart for Level 1

Leading Indicators for Level 1	Used as Basis for a Lagging Indicator?	Lagging Indicator(s)	Criterion Score or Concrete Product
1.1 The faculty and staff perceive the school environment as safe and orderly.			
1.2 Students, parents, and the community perceive the school environment as safe and orderly.			
1.3 Teachers have formal roles in the decision-making process regarding school initiatives.			
1.4 Teacher teams and collaborative groups regularly interact to address common issues regarding curriculum, assessment, instruction, and the achievement of all students.			
1.5 Teachers and staff have formal ways to provide input regarding the optimal functioning of the school.			
1.6 Students, parents, and the community have formal ways to provide input regarding the optimal functioning of the school.			
1.7 The success of the whole school, as well as individuals within the school, is appropriately acknowledged.			
1.8 The fiscal, operational, and technological resources of the school are managed in a way that directly supports teachers.			

Visit **marzanoresearch.com/reproducibles/leadership** *to download a reproducible version of this form.*

The principal determines that many of these injuries are the result of rules not being followed and that teacher assistants responsible for monitoring the playground do not have clear guidance as to what rules they are expected to enforce while on duty.

To address these issues, the principal designs the following lagging indicators (based on leading indicators 1.1 and 1.2) with criterion scores that will indicate his school has remedied the problem:

- Two or fewer incidents occur each month in which students' safety is compromised.
- Four or fewer incidents occur each month in which rules and procedures are not followed.

Then, he implements a system to meet the goals articulated in the lagging indicators. He forms a Playground Safety Committee, consisting of himself, the school nurse, the school psychologist, two classroom teachers (one primary, one intermediate), and two of the teacher assistants who monitor the playground. The committee designs a set of rules that clearly explain the expectations for student behavior on each piece of playground equipment and for team games played during recess periods. Additionally, they design a process to address students who consistently ignore playground expectations.

> **First offense:** Playground monitor explains what the student did to break a rule and gives the student a warning.
>
> **Second offense:** Student sits out for the rest of the recess period and fills out a reflection form (which is given to his classroom teacher) describing his behavior, the result of his behavior, and how he plans to make different choices in the future.
>
> **Third offense:** The student is sent to the office for a conference with the principal, and a phone call is made to a parent.

To help all students learn the new rules and expectations, several members of the committee create short video clips of students using playground equipment and playing team games correctly. These clips are shown during morning announcements over the course of the next week.

The principal tracks the incidence of rules being broken and playground injuries over the next three months. The first month, playground injuries drop from an average of two per day to an average of four per week, and, on average, one rule is broken each day. The second month, injuries are less frequent, occurring only once a week on average. Rules are only broken, on average, two times each week. During the third month, there are only two injuries during the entire month, and rules are broken only four times. Using these data, and data collected for the school's other lagging indicators, the principal determines that his school has achieved level 1 high reliability status.

Example 2

An elementary principal at a new school finds that staff members assign low ratings to leading indicator 1.3, "Teachers have formal roles in the decision-making process regarding school initiatives," on the leading indicator survey but very high survey responses for all other leading indicators. Based on subsequent conversations with teachers, she finds that they feel they have no say in important decisions, and some feel as if they are forced to implement initiatives that go against their fundamental beliefs about how children should be taught. To address this issue, the principal implements a decision-making process adapted from one used by religious organizations (such as the Quakers). During the decision-making process, staff members are asked to give their opinions and specify whether the issue at hand is a matter of preference or matter of conscience for them. Matters of preference are defined as those issues for which a person desires a certain outcome but could commit to live with and support the decision of the group. Matters of conscience are defined as those issues for which a person's values and beliefs are so strong that supporting a contrary decision would be difficult.

The principal uses the new decision-making process during a staff discussion of classroom multiage grouping. First, she explains what she thinks is the consensus of the group: students in kindergarten through second grade will be grouped together, and students in third through fifth grade will be grouped together. Next, she asks those who have opposing positions or concerns regarding the grouping structure to share their opinions and specify if they are matters of preference or matters of conscience.

All staff support the grouping structure except for one kindergarten teacher who indicates that she is opposed to the structure and that her opinion is a matter of conscience. "Kindergarten students are new to school, and they really need the opportunity to interact with same-age peers only as they learn to function in the classroom," she explains. Based on this teacher's opinion, the principal asks staff members to consider what she has said and puts the decision off until the next week. When the teachers convene for the next week's staff meeting, it quickly becomes apparent that a number of teachers have thought more about the issue and looked at research and agree with the kindergarten teacher's opinion. Therefore, the group decides to keep kindergarteners in a grade by themselves and only group first and second graders together in primary multiage classrooms.

Based on leading indicator 1.3, the principal creates a lagging indicator and criterion score that states, "Eighty percent of decisions that affect multiple staff members will be made using the Quaker decision-making process." Over the year, she keeps a file of meeting minutes and notes about all decisions made. Each month, she reviews the file to ensure that 80 percent of decisions affecting multiple staff members are made with those staff members' input and designation about whether the issue is a matter of preference or conscience for them.

Example 3

The principal of a large high school notices that survey responses for leading indicator 1.4, "Teacher teams and collaborative groups regularly interact to address common issues regarding curriculum, assessment, instruction, and the achievement of all students," are much lower than those for other indicators. The principal begins to work toward this leading indicator by forming an American history collaborative team to address a number of parent complaints he has recently received. Essentially, parents are concerned that students in different American history classes are learning different content and being asked to complete different projects depending on which teacher they have. Each teacher independently determines what he or she considers the most important content for his or her students to learn, what activities and assignments are best for learning that content, and what type of assessment activities are appropriate to test students' knowledge of the content.

To address the issue, and work toward enhancing the school's status on leading indicator 1.4, the principal asks the five American history teachers, a world history teacher, an American literature teacher, and one of the school's college guidance counselors to participate in this collaborative team. Together, they are responsible for identifying the content that is most important for students to learn, organizing that content into measurement topics and units, creating scales for each target learning goal, and writing common assessments that will be used to measure students' progress toward the learning goals. Additionally, the principal tasks the group with meeting once a week to discuss the content taught that week and the instructional strategies they used to deliver it. When assessments are given, the collaborative team analyzes the test data to determine areas of strength and areas that need to be improved. At the end of the year, the team analyzes data from districtwide assessments to revise the measurement topics and units for the next year.

To collect data about the process, the principal creates a lagging indicator and criterion score: "In each content area, collaborative teams will document the completion of at least two collaborative projects per year." The principal is responsible for helping collaborative teams form and facilitating their selection of appropriate projects. To document completion of a project, each team turns in meeting minutes and artifacts from its work together, along with a summary form that explains the purpose, process, and outcome of its project.

Quick Data for Level 1

After achieving high reliability status for level 1, school leaders can use quick data to continue to monitor the school's status. Here, we provide sample questions and incidents based on the leading indicators for level 1. We also provide suggestions for easy-to-collect quantitative data for level 1 and ways to acknowledge and celebrate success.

Quick Conversations

Questions for quick conversations at level 1 could include the following:

1.1 and 1.2	How safe has our school been lately?
1.1 and 1.2	How orderly has our school been lately?
1.3	Recently, to what extent have teachers had roles in making important decisions regarding the school?
1.4	Recently, to what extent have teacher teams and collaborative groups interacted to address common issues regarding curriculum, assessment, instruction, or student achievement?
1.5 and 1.6	Recently, to what extent have you had opportunities to provide input regarding the operations of the school?
1.7	Recently, to what extent have the accomplishments of the school or individuals been acknowledged and celebrated?
1.8	Recently, to what extent have teachers been provided with adequate time and resources to support their teaching?

Teachers from collaborative teams might ask one or more of these questions during a given interval of time. These data would be summarized on a regular (for example, monthly) basis.

Quick Observations

Quick observations can also be made for level 1 indicators. Such observations would focus on recent incidents that indicate the following:

- The school is a safe place.
- The school is an unsafe place.
- The school is an orderly place.
- The school is not an orderly place.
- Teachers have input into discussions.
- Teachers do not have input into discussions.
- Teacher teams and collaborative groups are interacting to address common issues regarding curriculum, assessment, instruction, or student achievement.
- Teacher teams and collaborative groups are not interacting to address common issues regarding curriculum, assessment, instruction, or student achievement.
- Teachers have opportunities to provide input into the operations of the school.
- Teachers do not have opportunities to provide input into the operations of the school.
- Students and parents have opportunities to provide input into the operations of the school.
- Students and parents do not have opportunities to provide input into the operations of the school.

- The accomplishments of the school or individuals have been acknowledged and celebrated.

- The accomplishments of the school or individuals have not been acknowledged and celebrated.

- Teachers have been provided with adequate time and resources to support their teaching.

- Teachers have not been provided with adequate time and resources to support their teaching.

These observations could be collected anecdotally (as in table I.4, page 10) and summarized in a narrative.

Easy-to-Collect Quantitative Data

In addition to quick conversation and quick observation data, a school should take advantage of easy-to-collect level 1 quantitative data that can be used to continuously monitor level 1 performance. Such data might include:

- Frequency counts of rule violations

- Frequency counts of discipline referrals and for which infractions—

  ◦ Detentions

  ◦ Suspensions (lunch suspensions, in-school suspensions, out-of-school suspensions)

  ◦ Expulsions

- School attendance data—

  ◦ Frequency counts of tardies

  ◦ Frequency counts of truancies

- Frequency counts of bullying incidents

- Frequency counts of parent communications expressing school safety concerns

- Frequency counts of student interactions with the guidance department related to school safety concerns

- Frequency counts of collaborative team meetings

- Frequency counts of teacher celebrations (teacher of the month, team of the month, and so on)

- District curriculum materials adoption schedule

- District, school, or parent-teacher organization budget item codes and amounts for purchased materials and resources

- Attendance records for teachers invited to leadership meetings

- Frequency counts of comments and suggestions submitted to the school's website

- Attendance records and minutes for parent focus groups

- The number of school community members who have contributed to the school constitution or code of conduct

- Periodic student "happiness" or attitudinal survey results (for example, see the Gallup Student Poll; Gallup, 2013)

- Periodic teacher "happiness" or attitudinal survey results

- Reports generated through online behavior management resources (such as www.ClassDojo.com)

Acknowledging and Celebrating Success

Periodically, quick data should be aggregated and reported. For example, once a month, school leaders would report the results from quick conversations, quick observations, and easy-to-collect quantitative data at a faculty meeting. School status would be discussed and success celebrated. The following vignette depicts how this might manifest.

> *Clear Creek High School achieved level 1 high reliability status at the end of the previous year and has been monitoring quick data related to that level since the beginning of the current year. At the school's monthly staff meeting, the leadership team presents quick data from the past month and celebrates successes. This month, the one-page summary passed out to staff members shows that quick conversation data were collected for three questions related to indicators of importance to the school. Results are indicated using bar graphs. Easy-to-collect quantitative data for level 1 are also summarized. This month's easy-to-collect data include frequency counts of tardies and rule violations. At the bottom of the page, a narrative summarizes quick observation data related to the same indicators. Dr. Rogers, the principal, gives teachers several minutes to read the results and then highlights celebrations.*
>
> *"Notice that we had no unsatisfactory answers for two of the questions in our quick conversation data!" he says.*
>
> *He asks two teachers to comment on how the school's success in those areas, along with the low number of tardies and rule violations, facilitated their personal success in the classroom before moving on to the quick observation data.*
>
> *"I want to specifically celebrate the group of teachers who facilitated the town hall meeting for students, parents, and community members last month. That meeting was cited multiple times in quick observation data as an incident that indicated that students and parents have opportunities to provide input into the operations of the school. Let's give them a round of applause!" he says.*
>
> *Staff members clap, and Dr. Rogers concludes by explaining what quick data the leadership team are planning to collect during the next month.*

Resources for Level 1

A school might use the following resources (listed chronologically; most recent first) to facilitate work at level 1:

- *Leaders of Learning: How District, School, and Classroom Leaders Improve Student Achievement* (DuFour & Marzano, 2011)
- *Effective Supervision: Supporting the Art and Science of Teaching* (Marzano, Frontier, & Livingston, 2011)
- *The Highly Engaged Classroom* (Marzano & Pickering, 2011)
- *On Excellence in Teaching* (Marzano, 2010b)
- *District Leadership That Works: Striking the Right Balance* (Marzano & Waters, 2009)
- *The Art and Science of Teaching: A Comprehensive Framework for Effective Instruction* (Marzano, 2007)
- *School Leadership That Works: From Research to Results* (Marzano et al., 2005)
- *Classroom Management That Works: Research-Based Strategies for Every Teacher* (Marzano, 2003a)
- *What Works in Schools: Translating Research Into Action* (Marzano, 2003b)

Other resources related to PLCs (the critical commitment for level 1), school safety, formal input, celebration and management, and other level 1 topics can also be used.

Chapter 2

Effective Teaching in Every Classroom

● ● ●

Level 2 addresses factors that relate to developing and maintaining effective instruction in every classroom. This is a central feature of effective schooling—the quality of teaching in classrooms. Level 2 has six leading indicators:

2.1 The school leader communicates a clear vision as to how instruction should be addressed in the school.

2.2 Support is provided to teachers to continually enhance their pedagogical skills through reflection and professional growth plans.

2.3 Predominant instructional practices throughout the school are known and monitored.

2.4 Teachers are provided with clear, ongoing evaluations of their pedagogical strengths and weaknesses that are based on multiple sources of data and are consistent with student achievement data.

2.5 Teachers are provided with job-embedded professional development that is directly related to their instructional growth goals.

2.6 Teachers have opportunities to observe and discuss effective teaching.

When a school reaches high reliability status for level 2, it can guarantee that quality teaching occurs in every classroom. Operationally, this means that variability in teacher quality within a school is quite low—every teacher uses effective instructional strategies.

Level 2 Short-Form Leading Indicator Survey

Figure 2.1 (page 38) presents a short-form leading indicator survey for level 2. This survey can be administered to faculty, staff, and administrators within a school. The short-form survey provides very general information about a school's level 2 status. For more specific information, long-form surveys should be used.

| 1: Strongly disagree | 2: Disagree | 3: Neither disagree nor agree |
| 4: Agree | 5: Strongly agree | N: N/A or don't know |

2.1 The school leader communicates a clear vision as to how instruction should be addressed in the school.	1	2	3	4	5	N
2.2 Support is provided to teachers to continually enhance their pedagogical skills through reflection and professional growth plans.	1	2	3	4	5	N
2.3 Predominant instructional practices throughout the school are known and monitored.	1	2	3	4	5	N
2.4 Teachers are provided with clear, ongoing evaluations of their pedagogical strengths and weaknesses that are based on multiple sources of data and are consistent with student achievement data.	1	2	3	4	5	N
2.5 Teachers are provided with job-embedded professional development that is directly related to their instructional growth goals.	1	2	3	4	5	N
2.6 Teachers have opportunities to observe and discuss effective teaching.	1	2	3	4	5	N

Figure 2.1: Level 2 short-form leading indicator survey.

Level 2 Long-Form Leading Indicator Surveys

The long-form leading indicator surveys for level 2 are designed to gather specific data from teachers and staff, administrators, students, and parents about a school's level 2 strengths and weaknesses. These surveys can and should be adapted by schools. Items could be deleted, added, or changed. Reproducibles 2.1–2.4 (pages 39–45) contain the surveys for level 2.

Reproducible 2.1: Level 2 Long-Form Leading Indicator Survey for Teachers and Staff

| 1: Strongly disagree | 2: Disagree | 3: Neither disagree nor agree |
| 4: Agree | 5: Strongly agree | N: N/A or don't know |

2.1 The school leader communicates a clear vision as to how instruction should be addressed in the school.	School leaders and teacher leaders have developed a written document articulating our schoolwide model of instruction.	1	2	3	4	5	N
	New teachers have professional development opportunities to learn about our schoolwide model of instruction.	1	2	3	4	5	N
	I can describe the major components of our schoolwide model of instruction.	1	2	3	4	5	N
	School leaders limit the number of new initiatives, prioritizing those related to our schoolwide model of instruction.	1	2	3	4	5	N
	Our school has a common language for talking about teaching and instruction.	1	2	3	4	5	N
	I use our schoolwide language of instruction in faculty and department meetings.	1	2	3	4	5	N
	I use our schoolwide language of instruction during PLC meetings.	1	2	3	4	5	N
	I use our schoolwide language of instruction in informal conversations.	1	2	3	4	5	N
2.2 Support is provided to teachers to continually enhance their pedagogical skills through reflection and professional growth plans.	I have written statements of my instructional growth goals.	1	2	3	4	5	N
	I keep track of my progress on my instructional growth goals.	1	2	3	4	5	N
	School leaders meet with me to discuss my instructional growth goals.	1	2	3	4	5	N
	I can describe my progress on my instructional growth goals.	1	2	3	4	5	N
	School leaders hire effective teachers.	1	2	3	4	5	N
	School leaders have a system in place to evaluate the hiring and selection process for new teachers.	1	2	3	4	5	N
	Our school has a new-teacher induction program.	1	2	3	4	5	N
	School leaders have a system in place to evaluate and revise our new-teacher induction program.	1	2	3	4	5	N
	School leaders retain effective teachers.	1	2	3	4	5	N
	School leaders can provide evaluation results, growth plans, and evidence of support for any struggling teachers.	1	2	3	4	5	N
2.3 Predominant instructional practices throughout the school are known and monitored.	Data from walkthroughs at our school are aggregated to show our school's predominant instructional practices.	1	2	3	4	5	N
	School leaders can describe our school's predominant instructional practices.	1	2	3	4	5	N
	I can describe our school's predominant instructional practices.	1	2	3	4	5	N
	School leaders give me forthright feedback about my instructional practices.	1	2	3	4	5	N
	School leaders can describe effective practices and problems of practice in our school.	1	2	3	4	5	N

page 1 of 2

2.4 Teachers are provided with clear, ongoing evaluations of their pedagogical strengths and weaknesses that are based on multiple sources of data and are consistent with student achievement data.	School leaders use highly specific rubrics to give me accurate feedback about my pedagogical strengths and weaknesses.	1	2	3	4	5	N
	School leaders use multiple sources of information to give me feedback and evaluate me, including direct observation, teacher self-reports, video analysis, student reports, and peer feedback from other teachers.	1	2	3	4	5	N
	School leaders regularly talk to me about the evaluation data they have collected for me.	1	2	3	4	5	N
	School leaders observe me frequently.	1	2	3	4	5	N
	School leaders give me feedback frequently.	1	2	3	4	5	N
	I can explain which of my instructional strategies have the strongest and weakest relationships to student achievement.	1	2	3	4	5	N
2.5 Teachers are provided with job-embedded professional development that is directly related to their instructional growth goals.	Online professional development courses and resources that are relevant to my instructional growth goals are available to me.	1	2	3	4	5	N
	Teacher-led professional development that is relevant to my instructional growth goals is available to me.	1	2	3	4	5	N
	Instructional coaching relevant to my instructional growth goals is available to me.	1	2	3	4	5	N
	School leaders collect data about how effective professional development is in improving teacher practices.	1	2	3	4	5	N
	I can describe how the available professional development supports achievement of my instructional growth goals.	1	2	3	4	5	N
2.6 Teachers have opportunities to observe and discuss effective teaching.	I have opportunities to engage in instructional rounds.	1	2	3	4	5	N
	I have opportunities to view and discuss video examples of effective teaching.	1	2	3	4	5	N
	I have regular times to meet with other teachers to discuss effective instructional practices (for example, lesson study).	1	2	3	4	5	N
	I have opportunities to observe and discuss effective teaching via technology (for example, virtual coaching or online discussions).	1	2	3	4	5	N
	We regularly discuss instructional practices at faculty and department meetings.	1	2	3	4	5	N
	We regularly view and discuss video examples of effective teaching at faculty and department meetings.	1	2	3	4	5	N
	School leaders have information available about teachers' participation in opportunities to observe and discuss effective teaching.	1	2	3	4	5	N
	School leaders have information available about teachers' participation in virtual discussions on effective teaching.	1	2	3	4	5	N

Reproducible 2.2: Level 2 Long-Form Leading Indicator Survey for Administrators

| 1: Strongly disagree | 2: Disagree | 3: Neither disagree nor agree |
| 4: Agree | 5: Strongly agree | N: N/A or don't know |

2.1 The school leader communicates a clear vision as to how instruction should be addressed in the school.	Teacher leaders and I have developed a written document articulating our schoolwide model of instruction.	1	2	3	4	5	N
	New teachers have professional development opportunities to learn about our schoolwide model of instruction.	1	2	3	4	5	N
	I can describe the major components of our schoolwide model of instruction.	1	2	3	4	5	N
	I limit the number of new initiatives, prioritizing those related to our schoolwide model of instruction.	1	2	3	4	5	N
	Our school has a common language for talking about teaching and instruction.	1	2	3	4	5	N
	I use our schoolwide language of instruction in faculty and department meetings.	1	2	3	4	5	N
	I use our schoolwide language of instruction during PLC meetings.	1	2	3	4	5	N
	I use our schoolwide language of instruction in informal conversations.	1	2	3	4	5	N
2.2 Support is provided to teachers to continually enhance their pedagogical skills through reflection and professional growth plans.	Teachers have written statements of their instructional growth goals.	1	2	3	4	5	N
	Teachers keep track of their progress on their instructional growth goals.	1	2	3	4	5	N
	I meet with teachers to discuss their instructional growth goals.	1	2	3	4	5	N
	Teachers can describe their progress on their instructional growth goals.	1	2	3	4	5	N
	I hire effective teachers.	1	2	3	4	5	N
	There is a system in place to evaluate the hiring and selection process for new teachers.	1	2	3	4	5	N
	Our school has a new-teacher induction program.	1	2	3	4	5	N
	There is a system in place to evaluate and revise our new-teacher induction program.	1	2	3	4	5	N
	I retain effective teachers.	1	2	3	4	5	N
	I can provide evaluation results, growth plans, and evidence of support for any struggling teachers.	1	2	3	4	5	N
2.3 Predominant instructional practices throughout the school are known and monitored.	Data from walkthroughs at our school are aggregated to show our school's predominant instructional practices.	1	2	3	4	5	N
	I can describe our school's predominant instructional practices.	1	2	3	4	5	N
	Teachers can describe our school's predominant instructional practices.	1	2	3	4	5	N
	I give teachers forthright feedback about their instructional practices.	1	2	3	4	5	N
	I can describe effective practices and problems of practice in our school.	1	2	3	4	5	N

page 1 of 2

2.4 Teachers are provided with clear, ongoing evaluations of their pedagogical strengths and weaknesses that are based on multiple sources of data and are consistent with student achievement data.	I use highly specific rubrics to give teachers accurate feedback about their pedagogical strengths and weaknesses.	1	2	3	4	5	N
	I use multiple sources of information to give teachers feedback and evaluate them, including direct observation, teacher self-reports, video analysis, student reports, and peer feedback from other teachers.	1	2	3	4	5	N
	I regularly talk to teachers about the evaluation data I have collected for them.	1	2	3	4	5	N
	I observe teachers frequently.	1	2	3	4	5	N
	I give teachers feedback frequently.	1	2	3	4	5	N
	Teachers can explain which of their instructional strategies have the strongest and weakest relationships to student achievement.	1	2	3	4	5	N
2.5 Teachers are provided with job-embedded professional development that is directly related to their instructional growth goals.	Online professional development courses and resources that are relevant to teachers' instructional growth goals are available to them.	1	2	3	4	5	N
	Teacher-led professional development relevant to teachers' instructional growth goals is available to them.	1	2	3	4	5	N
	Instructional coaching relevant to teachers' instructional growth goals is available to them.	1	2	3	4	5	N
	I collect data about how effective professional development is in improving teacher practices.	1	2	3	4	5	N
	Teachers can describe how the available professional development supports achievement of their instructional growth goals.	1	2	3	4	5	N
2.6 Teachers have opportunities to observe and discuss effective teaching.	Teachers have opportunities to engage in instructional rounds.	1	2	3	4	5	N
	Teachers have opportunities to view and discuss video examples of effective teaching.	1	2	3	4	5	N
	Teachers have regular times to meet with other teachers to discuss effective instructional practices (for example, lesson study).	1	2	3	4	5	N
	Teachers have opportunities to observe and discuss effective teaching via technology (for example, virtual coaching or online discussions).	1	2	3	4	5	N
	We regularly discuss instructional practices at faculty and department meetings.	1	2	3	4	5	N
	We regularly view and discuss video examples of effective teaching at faculty and department meetings.	1	2	3	4	5	N
	I make information available about teachers' participation in opportunities to observe and discuss effective teaching.	1	2	3	4	5	N
	I make information available about teachers' participation in virtual discussions about effective teaching.	1	2	3	4	5	N

page 2 of 2

Reproducible 2.3: Level 2 Long-Form Leading Indicator Survey for Students

| 1: Strongly disagree | 2: Disagree | 3: Neither disagree nor agree |
| 4: Agree | 5: Strongly agree | N: N/A or don't know |

2.1 The school leader communicates a clear vision as to how instruction should be addressed in the school.	My teachers use the same language and words to talk about how they teach and the activities we do in class.	1	2	3	4	5	N
2.2 Support is provided to teachers to continually enhance their pedagogical skills through reflection and professional growth plans.	Teachers at my school are good teachers.	1	2	3	4	5	N
	My teachers have goals to help them become better teachers.	1	2	3	4	5	N
	New teachers at my school take classes to help them become better teachers.	1	2	3	4	5	N
	Good teachers stay at my school.	1	2	3	4	5	N
	If a teacher is having trouble teaching, my school's leaders help him or her.	1	2	3	4	5	N
2.3 Predominant instructional practices throughout the school are known and monitored.	My school's leaders observe my teachers on a regular basis.	1	2	3	4	5	N
2.4 Teachers are provided with clear, ongoing evaluations of their pedagogical strengths and weaknesses that are based on multiple sources of data and are consistent with student achievement data.	My teachers can explain how the activities and strategies they use help me learn.	1	2	3	4	5	N
	My school's leaders talk to my teachers about how to be better teachers.	1	2	3	4	5	N
2.5 Teachers are provided with job-embedded professional development that is directly related to their instructional growth goals.	My teachers spend time learning how to be better teachers.	1	2	3	4	5	N
	My teachers have coaches who come and watch them teach.	1	2	3	4	5	N
	My teachers record their teaching on video to watch later.	1	2	3	4	5	N
2.6 Teachers have opportunities to observe and discuss effective teaching.	Groups of teachers come to observe some of my teachers.	1	2	3	4	5	N
	Teachers in my school meet to talk about how to be better teachers.	1	2	3	4	5	N

Reproducible 2.4: Level 2 Long-Form Leading Indicator Survey for Parents

| 1: Strongly disagree | 2: Disagree | 3: Neither disagree nor agree |
| 4: Agree | 5: Strongly agree | N: N/A or don't know |

		1	2	3	4	5	N
2.1 The school leader communicates a clear vision as to how instruction should be addressed in the school.	My child's school has a schoolwide model of instruction.	1	2	3	4	5	N
	Teachers and leaders at my child's school can describe and explain the schoolwide model of instruction.	1	2	3	4	5	N
	New teachers receive training in the schoolwide model of instruction at my child's school.	1	2	3	4	5	N
	The leaders of my child's school limit the number of new initiatives at the school, prioritizing those related to the schoolwide model of instruction.	1	2	3	4	5	N
	Teachers and leaders at my child's school use a common language of instruction to talk to me about how teachers teach.	1	2	3	4	5	N
2.2 Support is provided to teachers to continually enhance their pedagogical skills through reflection and professional growth plans.	The teachers at my child's school have growth goals to improve their instruction.	1	2	3	4	5	N
	The leaders of my child's school hire effective teachers.	1	2	3	4	5	N
	New teachers at my child's school complete a new-teacher induction program.	1	2	3	4	5	N
	The leaders of my child's school retain effective teachers.	1	2	3	4	5	N
	The leaders of my child's school provide support for any struggling teachers.	1	2	3	4	5	N
2.3 Predominant instructional practices throughout the school are known and monitored.	The leaders of my child's school regularly observe teachers teaching.	1	2	3	4	5	N
	The leaders of my child's school can describe the predominant instructional practices used by teachers in the school.	1	2	3	4	5	N
	The leaders of my child's school can describe effective practices and problems of practice in the school.	1	2	3	4	5	N
2.4 Teachers are provided with clear, ongoing evaluations of their pedagogical strengths and weaknesses that are based on multiple sources of data and are consistent with student achievement data.	The leaders of my child's school frequently observe teachers and give them feedback about the effectiveness of their instruction.	1	2	3	4	5	N
	Teachers at my child's school can explain which of their instructional strategies have the strongest and weakest relationships to student achievement.	1	2	3	4	5	N

page 1 of 2

2.5 Teachers are provided with job-embedded professional development that is directly related to their instructional growth goals.	Teachers at my child's school have regular opportunities to receive professional development training.	1	2	3	4	5	N
	Teachers at my child's school have instructional growth goals.	1	2	3	4	5	N
	Teachers at my child's school receive coaching to help them achieve their instructional growth goals.	1	2	3	4	5	N
2.6 Teachers have opportunities to observe and discuss effective teaching.	Groups of teachers regularly observe exemplary teachers at my child's school.	1	2	3	4	5	N
	Teachers at my child's school view and discuss video examples of exemplary teaching.	1	2	3	4	5	N
	Teachers at my child's school meet together regularly to discuss effective teaching practices.	1	2	3	4	5	N

A Handbook for High Reliability Schools © 2014 Marzano Research • marzanoresearch.com

Once teachers, staff members, administrators, students, and parents have completed the appropriate surveys from reproducibles 2.1–2.4, school leaders compile the results to determine what leading indicators they may need to work on relative to their school's instructional framework. For example, after examining survey results for level 2, school leaders see that faculty and staff responses to leading indicator 2.6, "Teachers have opportunities to observe and discuss effective teaching," are consistently lower than responses to other leading indicators. To address this area, the leaders implement instructional rounds. This approach is one element of an evaluation system whose primary focus is teacher development, the critical commitment for level 2.

Level 2 Critical Commitment

Clearly, teacher evaluation is one of the major initiatives of the second decade of the 21st century. Indeed, it is such a robust movement that it can be used to address every issue relative to level 2 status, but to do so it must have a primary focus on teacher development. As Marzano noted in a 2012 article, "The Two Purposes of Teacher Evaluation," states, districts, and schools across the United States should ask themselves, "Is the purpose of teacher evaluation primarily measurement or development?"

In the article, Marzano (2012b) reported the results of an informal survey administered to over three thousand K–12 educators. That survey employed a simple scale with values ranging from 1 to 5. The results from the survey are depicted in table 2.1.

Table 2.1: Results From Informal Survey Regarding the Purposes of Teacher Evaluation

The purpose of teacher evaluation should be . . .	Results
5: Completely development	2%
4: Both, but development is more important	76%
3: Development and measurement are equally important	20%
2: Both, but measurement is more important	2%
1: Completely measurement	0%

As indicated in table 2.1, the vast majority of those who responded to the informal survey thought both were important but favored development as the primary purpose of teacher evaluation. We believe that a teacher evaluation system focused on development has three characteristics: (1) the system is comprehensive and specific, (2) the system includes a developmental scale, and (3) the system acknowledges and supports growth.

The System Is Comprehensive and Specific

Comprehensive means the system includes all those elements that research has identified as associated with student achievement. *Specific* means the system identifies classroom strategies and behaviors at a granular level. Here, we present an example framework.

The model was first articulated in the book *The Art and Science of Teaching* (Marzano, 2007) and later expanded in the book *Effective Supervision* (Marzano et al., 2011). Other books have described the model's implications for teachers' self-analysis and reflection (*Becoming a Reflective Teacher*, Marzano, 2012a) as well as the implications of the model for coaching teachers (*Coaching Classroom Instruction*, Marzano & Simms, 2013a). In its entirety, the model addresses the domains of classroom instruction, planning and preparing, teacher self-reflection, and collegiality and professionalism.

The forty-one elements in the framework (see table 2.2) are categorized according to the type of lesson segment in which they normally occur—those involving routine events, those addressing content, and those enacted on the spot. Such a comprehensive and detailed listing of instructional strategies makes perfect sense in the context of a teacher evaluation system focused on development.

An evaluation system designed primarily for measurement would not need to be as robust. In fact, many of the elements in table 2.2 are unnecessary if the sole purpose of teacher evaluation is measurement. This is because some of the strategy areas correlate with student achievement but are not required to be effective in the classroom. For example, consider element 25, using academic games, which is certainly a useful tool in enhancing student achievement (Hattie, 2009; Walberg, 1999). However, every teacher does not have to use academic games. Indeed, a teacher can produce dramatic gains in student learning without using games at all. A teacher evaluation system focused on measurement alone would only involve those elements that cut across all grade levels, all subjects, and all types of students. In *The Art and Science of Teaching* model, there are fifteen such elements, which are bolded in table 2.2. However, it is important to note that these elements would not address the fine-tuned granular levels of behavior that distinguish true experts in the classroom from everyone else.

As Nalini Ambady and Robert Rosenthal (1992) noted, expertise occurs in "thin slices of behavior" (p. 257). To develop those thin slices of behavior characteristic of experts, teachers need feedback on all forty-one elements. Using that feedback, teachers can identify areas of strength and weakness and then systematically begin improving their areas of weakness.

Table 2.2: *The Art and Science of Teaching* Framework

I. Lesson Segments Involving Routine Events
A. *What will I do to establish and communicate learning goals, track student progress, and celebrate success?*
1. Providing clear learning goals and scales (rubrics)
2. Tracking student progress
3. Celebrating success
B. *What will I do to establish and maintain classroom rules and procedures?*
4. Establishing and maintaining classroom rules and procedures
5. Organizing the physical layout of the classroom
II. Lesson Segments Addressing Content
C. *What will I do to help students effectively interact with new knowledge?*
6. Identifying critical information
7. Organizing students to interact with new knowledge
8. Previewing new content
9. Chunking content into "digestible bites"
10. Helping students process new information
11. Helping students elaborate on new information
12. Helping students record and represent knowledge
13. Helping students reflect on their learning

D. *What will I do to help students practice and deepen their understanding of new knowledge?*
14. Reviewing content
15. Organizing students to practice and deepen knowledge
16. Using homework
17. Helping students examine similarities and differences
18. Helping students examine errors in reasoning
19. Helping students practice skills, strategies, and processes
20. Helping students revise knowledge
E. *What will I do to help students generate and test hypotheses about new knowledge?*
21. Organizing students for cognitively complex tasks
22. Engaging students in cognitively complex tasks involving hypothesis generation and testing
23. Providing resources and guidance

III. Lesson Segments Enacted on the Spot

F. *What will I do to engage students?*
24. Noticing and reacting when students are not engaged
25. Using academic games
26. Managing response rates during questioning
27. Using physical movement
28. Maintaining a lively pace
29. Demonstrating intensity and enthusiasm
30. Using friendly controversy
31. Providing opportunities for students to talk about themselves
32. Presenting unusual or intriguing information
G. *What will I do to recognize and acknowledge adherence or lack of adherence to rules and procedures?*
33. Demonstrating "withitness"
34. Applying consequences for lack of adherence to rules and procedures
35. Acknowledging adherence to rules and procedures
H. *What will I do to establish and maintain effective relationships with students?*
36. Understanding students' interests and backgrounds
37. Using verbal and nonverbal behaviors that indicate affection for students
38. Displaying objectivity and control
I. *What will I do to communicate high expectations for all students?*
39. Demonstrating value and respect for low-expectancy students
40. Asking questions of low-expectancy students
41. Probing incorrect answers with low-expectancy students

Source: Adapted from Marzano & Simms, 2013a, pp. 19–21.

Each of the forty-one elements has substantial research supporting its efficacy (see Marzano, 2007), and we believe the model accurately represents the diversity of strategies that highly effective teachers employ.

The System Includes a Developmental Scale

The second characteristic of a teacher evaluation system that focuses on development is that it employs a scale or rubric teachers can use to guide and track their skill development. Such a scale would articulate developmental levels, such as those shown in table 2.3.

Table 2.3: Developmental Scale

Innovating (4)	Applying (3)	Developing (2)	Beginning (1)	Not Using (0)
The teacher adapts or creates a new version of the strategy or behavior for unique student needs and situations.	The teacher uses the strategy or behavior and monitors the extent to which it affects student outcomes.	The teacher uses the strategy or behavior but does so in a somewhat mechanistic way.	The teacher uses the strategy or behavior incorrectly or with parts missing.	The teacher should use the strategy or behavior but does not.

Source: Marzano, 2012a, p. 37.

Not using indicates that a teacher is not aware of a particular strategy or is aware of it but has not tried it in his or her classroom. For example, if a teacher were unaware of strategies for engaging students in friendly controversy (element 30 in table 2.2), he or she would be at the *not using* level.

At the *beginning* level, a teacher knows about a strategy and uses it in the classroom but exhibits errors or omissions in its execution. For example, a teacher using the strategy of friendly controversy is at the beginning level if he or she simply asks students to state their opinions about a topic. Although students are performing one component of the strategy—stating their opinions—they are not supporting their opinions with evidence or disagreeing respectfully with others, which are also important components of the strategy.

At the *developing* level, the teacher uses the strategy without significant errors or omissions and with relative fluency. For example, a teacher using friendly controversy is at the developing level if he or she creates guidelines to prevent negativity during friendly controversy activities, asks students to express their opinions about topics and issues, and then asks students to defend their opinions about topics and issues.

At the *applying* level, a teacher not only executes a strategy with fluency but also monitors the class to ensure that the strategy is having its desired effect. A teacher using the friendly controversy strategy at the applying level would verify that students are backing up their opinions with evidence and disagreeing in a controlled and respectful manner. At the applying level and above, a strategy has the potential to produce large gains in student learning.

Finally, at the *innovating* level, the teacher monitors the class to ensure that a strategy is having its desired effect with the majority of students and makes necessary adaptations to ensure that all student populations are experiencing the strategy's positive effects. To reach all students, a teacher will most likely have to make adaptations for English learners (ELs) or for students who are lacking in important background knowledge for the topic being addressed. In other words, a teacher at the innovating level is effectively differentiating instruction (Tomlinson & Imbeau, 2010).

The scale in table 2.3 is specifically designed with teacher development in mind. It enables teachers (commonly with the aid of a supervisor or instructional coach) to pinpoint their current level of performance for a specific strategy, set goals for operating at higher levels within a given period of time, and then achieve those goals as part of their personal growth plan.

The System Acknowledges and Supports Growth

The third characteristic of an evaluation system focused on teacher development is that it explicitly acknowledges and rewards teacher growth. Each year, teachers identify elements (from the forty-one listed in table 2.2, page 47) on which to improve. Then they chart their progress on the selected elements, or growth goals, throughout the year. In addition to being assigned *status scores* that indicate their current level of proficiency with the various elements within the model, teachers are assigned *growth scores* based on the extent to which they achieve their goals. For example, assume a teacher selects three elements from table 2.2 to improve on over the year. Attaining his or her growth goals for all three elements would earn the highest growth score, attaining two of three goals would earn the next highest growth score, and so on. At the end of the year, teachers would have two summative scores: an overall status score and an overall growth score. Both of these scores would be considered when assigning teachers to a summative category of effectiveness regarding their teaching at the end of the year (for example, *highly effective*, *effective*, *developing*, or *unsatisfactory*). Such a system communicates to teachers that the school expects—and rewards—continuous improvement.

A teacher evaluation system that focuses on teacher development can be highly instrumental in satisfying the six leading indicators for level 2. For example, having a comprehensive, specific system greatly facilitates attainment of a clear vision of instruction (leading indicator 2.1) and clear and ongoing evaluations of teachers' pedagogical strengths and weaknesses (leading indicator 2.4). Use of a developmental scale helps teachers enhance their pedagogical skills (leading indicator 2.2) and provides evidence regarding the predominant instructional practices used throughout the school (leading indicator 2.3). Acknowledging and supporting growth naturally leads to a school providing job-embedded professional development (leading indicator 2.5) and providing opportunities for teachers to observe and discuss effective teaching (leading indicator 2.6).

Level 2 Lagging Indicators

As at level 1, lagging indicators (and corresponding criterion scores) provide evidence that a school has reached a specific level of reliability, especially for areas initially perceived as problematic. To illustrate how lagging indicators developed from level 2 leading indicators might look, consider the following examples:

- A document describing the school's instructional model is available.
- Survey data indicate that 100 percent of teachers are well aware of the school's instructional model and their status within that model.
- Eighty percent of teachers hired by the school leaders receive summative scores in the *effective* or *highly effective* range within three years.
- Teacher turnover is limited to two or fewer teachers per year.
- On average, teachers improve two or more levels of the scale for each of their growth goals each year.
- The modal summative score of teachers in the school is *effective* or higher.
- Any teacher who received a summative score of less than *effective* the previous year has a detailed, written growth plan.
- Survey data indicate 90 percent or higher agreement that the school in general and the evaluation system in particular are designed to help teachers improve their pedagogical skills.
- All teachers who fail to meet their goals after completing a detailed, written growth plan over the course of multiple years are counseled out of the profession or terminated in extreme cases.
- The correlation between teacher evaluation scores and state-level value-added measures of student learning is 0.40 or higher.

While there is no set number of lagging indicators a school should use, information gleaned from the leading indicator surveys can identify areas of perceived weakness for which lagging indicators are especially important. A chart like the one in table 2.4 can facilitate the process of moving from leading indicators to lagging indicators.

Table 2.4: Lagging Indicator Determination Chart for Level 2

Leading Indicators for Level 2	Used as Basis for a Lagging Indicator?	Lagging Indicator(s)	Criterion Score or Concrete Product
2.1 The school leader communicates a clear vision as to how instruction should be addressed in the school.			
2.2 Support is provided to teachers to continually enhance their pedagogical skills through reflection and professional growth plans.			
2.3 Predominant instructional practices throughout the school are known and monitored.			
2.4 Teachers are provided with clear, ongoing evaluations of their pedagogical strengths and weaknesses that are based on multiple sources of data and are consistent with student achievement data.			
2.5 Teachers are provided with job-embedded professional development that is directly related to their instructional growth goals.			
2.6 Teachers have opportunities to observe and discuss effective teaching.			

*Visit **marzanoresearch.com/reproducibles/leadership** to download a reproducible version of this form.*

School leaders create lagging indicators for those areas that are important to the school. Here, we offer several examples of how school leaders might carry this out.

Example 1

While evaluating level 2 survey responses from her staff, a high school principal notices that teacher responses to leading indicator 2.1, "The school leader communicates a clear vision as to how instruction should be addressed in the school," are low. Further conversations with lead teachers in each department reveal that teachers look to their department heads, rather than the principal, for direction about instructional strategies to use and how to improve their practice. Because each department head subscribes to a slightly different model of instruction, this results in a wide variety of approaches to instruction throughout the school.

To remedy the situation, the principal works with department heads to identify a common model and language of instruction that everyone in the school will use to talk about instructional strategies and techniques that should be used in the classroom. Additionally, the principal specifies that teachers should choose their growth goals each year directly from the model of instruction. After training the department heads in the new model, the principal trains all teachers in it. Part of the training involves creating a one-page document that summarizes all of the elements and domains of effective teaching, as specified in the model of instruction. The document is then posted in the teachers' workroom, above copiers around the school, and in the teachers' lounge. Observations and evaluations are also aligned to the model.

To measure the school's progress, the principal designs the following lagging indicator and criterion score: "Surveys show that 95 percent of staff members can accurately describe the school's model of instruction." The principal designs an email survey that is sent to teachers once a month asking questions about the school's model of instruction, and she tracks the percentage of staff who correctly answer the questions on the survey. The first month, only 60 percent of staff members correctly answer all of the questions about the model. The second month, the number rises to 75 percent. By the fifth month, 98 percent of staff members respond correctly when asked questions about the school's model of instruction.

Example 2

After analyzing level 2 survey data, the principal of an elementary school finds that staff responses to leading indicator 2.2, "Support is provided to teachers to continually enhance their pedagogical skills through reflection and professional growth plans," are significantly lower than those for other leading indicators. Through conversations with teachers, the principal realizes that teachers do not feel encouraged to reflect on their practice except when they are evaluated. They feel as if the principal takes responsibility to point out problems of practice, but they do not feel personally responsible for their growth.

In response, the principal implements self-audits at the beginning of the next quarter. Teachers rate themselves for each element of the school's model of instruction using a five-point scale. Then, they select a growth goal from among those elements for which they rated themselves at the *beginning* (1) or *not using* (0) level. Each week, the principal sends out a reflection form to all teachers. They reflect on their practice over the past week and note if they feel they've moved to a higher level of the scale. The principal incorporates these weekly reflections into observations and evaluation conferences.

To measure the school's progress, the principal designs the following lagging indicator and criterion score: "All teachers in the school will complete a self-audit each quarter, set at least one growth goal per quarter, and reflect on that goal weekly." Although all teachers complete the self-audit and select a growth goal, only about half of the teachers complete the reflection form and return it to the principal the next week. The second week, again, only half of the teachers return the reflection form. To remedy the situation, the principal decides to hold a drawing each week for free dinner at a local restaurant. Only those who turn in reflection forms for the week are entered into the drawing. The third week, 90 percent of teachers turn in their forms. The principal follows up with the few teachers who are still not turning in their forms, and by the fourth week, all teachers turn in their forms.

Example 3

To her surprise, the principal of a middle school finds that responses for leading indicator 2.5, "Teachers are provided with job-embedded professional development that is directly related to their instructional growth goals," are remarkably low in her school. She is shocked; for the past two years, she has worked specifically on providing high-quality professional development for teachers in her school. On every staff development day, she makes sure that she has an expert from the district or an outside consultant to present to teachers. Perplexed, she asks several teachers about their responses. Each teacher's answer is the same: "Professional development is provided, but it has nothing to do with our growth goals." One teacher says, "I feel like we're getting all this information, but we can't use any of it today in our classrooms. The things I need to know, I have to find on my own, plus I have to manage a whole bunch of information that seems irrelevant." In response to this information, the principal decides to take a different approach to professional development.

First, she creates a spreadsheet showing every teacher in the school and his or her growth goals for the fall, winter, and spring trimesters. Then, she groups teachers together who are working on similar goals at the same time. Finally, she meets with each group to determine what professional development opportunities would be most meaningful to those teachers and does her best to accommodate their requests. This means that professional development begins to look different in her school. Instead of all teachers receiving the same professional development in a whole group, small groups meet with experts (usually from the district, another school, or the same school) to discuss what they can do that day or week to pursue their goals.

The principal creates a lagging indicator and criterion score to measure progress toward differentiated and targeted professional development: "All teachers will report that they have received professional development within the past month that is directly related to their current growth goal." Each month, the principal asks teachers if the professional development they received that month was directly relevant to their growth goals. The first month, all but three teachers answer yes. The principal meets with the three teachers who answered no to adjust their situation. One moves to a different group, and the other two request to be allowed to do a book study together as their professional development. The second month, all teachers report that the professional development they received was directly relevant to their goals. During the third month, however, several teachers report that their professional development is no longer relevant. The principal makes adjustments until all teachers again report that, yes, their professional development is appropriate and timely.

Quick Data for Level 2

Once high reliability status has been achieved for level 2, continuous monitoring can be accomplished by using quick conversations, quick observations, and easy-to-collect quantitative data. We also provide suggestions for ways to acknowledge and celebrate success.

Quick Conversations

Questions for quick conversations at level 2 might include the following:

2.1 Recently, to what extent have teachers demonstrated a clear understanding of the school's instructional framework?

2.2 Recently, to what extent have teachers been provided with support to continually enhance their pedagogical skills through reflection and professional growth plans?

2.3 Recently, to what extent have predominant instructional practices throughout the school been monitored?

2.4 Recently, to what extent have teachers been provided with clear, ongoing evaluations of their pedagogical strengths and weaknesses based on multiple sources of data?

2.5 Recently, to what extent have teachers been provided with job-embedded professional development that is directly related to their instructional growth goals?

2.6 Recently, to what extent have teachers had opportunities to observe and discuss effective teaching?

As explained previously, these questions are based on leading indicators, but school leaders can also design questions based on items not explicit in the leading indicators. Again, teachers from collaborative teams could ask one or more of these questions during a given interval of time. These data would be summarized, perhaps once per month.

Quick Observations

Additionally, quick observations could also be made for level 2 indicators. Such observations should focus on recent incidents that indicate the following:

- A clear vision of instruction is present in the school.
- A clear vision of instruction is not present in the school.
- Teachers have been provided with support to continually enhance their pedagogical skills through reflection and professional growth plans.
- Teachers have not been provided with support to continually enhance their pedagogical skills through reflection and professional growth plans.
- Predominant instructional practices throughout the school are known and monitored.
- Predominant instructional practices throughout the school are not known and monitored.
- Teachers are provided with clear, ongoing evaluations of their pedagogical strengths and weaknesses based on multiple sources of data.
- Teachers are not provided with clear, ongoing evaluations of their pedagogical strengths and weaknesses based on multiple sources of data.
- Teachers are provided with job-embedded professional development that is directly related to their instructional growth goals.
- Teachers are not provided with job-embedded professional development that is directly related to their instructional growth goals.
- Teachers have opportunities to observe and discuss effective teaching.
- Teachers do not have opportunities to observe and discuss effective teaching.

Observation data can be collected anecdotally (as in table I.4, page 10) and summarized in a short narrative.

Easy-to-Collect Quantitative Data

In addition to quick conversations and quick observations, a school should take advantage of easy-to-collect level 2 quantitative data in order to continuously monitor level 2 performance. Such data might include:

- Average teacher scores on teacher evaluation protocols
- Charts showing the relationship between teacher evaluation scores and student achievement

- Teacher satisfaction scores for professional development workshops
- Teacher requests for professional development connected to the instructional framework (for example, "I want to attend this workshop because it relates to my growth goal of noticing and reacting when students are not engaged")
- Walkthrough data (from administrators) connected directly to the instructional model
- Teacher survey results indicating professional development needs
- Data related to instructional rounds—
  - Schedule of instructional rounds and participating teachers
  - Copies of feedback provided to teachers who were observed for instructional rounds
  - Average number of instructional rounds that teachers engage in during the course of the school year
- Student focus group data about instructional practices used by teachers
- Focused walkthrough observations looking for specific instructional practices
- Teacher attendance data related to professional development opportunities
- Survey results showing the relationship between professional development workshop content and improved classroom instructional practice

Acknowledging and Celebrating Success

Periodically, the quick data gathered for level 2 should be reported and celebrated. It is important to note that data from all levels for which high reliability status has been obtained are systematically acknowledged and celebrated, as shown in the following vignette.

Fox Valley Elementary School achieved level 2 high reliability status in the fall and has been continuously monitoring data since then to prevent problems and address errors. At the school's weekly staff meeting, the principal, Ms. O'Donnell, acknowledges and celebrates some aspect of the school's quick data, both for level 2 and for level 1. She displays bar graphs with quick conversation data for a level 1 question, a level 2 question, and some easy-to-collect quantitative data (such as a chart showing the relationship between teacher evaluation scores and student achievement) as teachers come in, and she begins the meeting by telling a short story based on quick data. Today, the featured quick conversation questions are:

- *To what extent have teachers been provided with adequate time and resources to support their teaching (level 1)?*

- *To what extent do teachers have opportunities to observe and discuss effective teaching (level 2)?*

The graphs show that 60 percent of responses to the first question were coded as adequate, and 40 percent were coded as excellent. Responses to the second question were 70 percent adequate and 30 percent excellent. Ms. O'Donnell draws teachers' attention to these results and asks those teachers who have been observed during instructional rounds to stand for a round of applause to thank them for opening their classrooms to observers.

"These teachers are an integral part of our school's ability to provide opportunities for teachers to observe and discuss effective teaching," says Ms. O'Donnell.

After displaying quantitative data that show a 10 percent rise in teacher satisfaction scores from professional development workshops at the school, she goes on to tell the story of an incident from quick observation data that indicated both that teacher teams were interacting to address common issues regarding instruction and that predominant instructional practices throughout the school were known and monitored. She uses specific teachers' names in the story and celebrates all teachers' commitment to the school's high reliability status at levels 1 and 2.

Resources for Level 2

A school might use the following resources (listed chronologically; most recent first) to facilitate work at level 2:

- *Questioning Sequences in the Classroom* (Marzano & Simms, 2014)
- *Enhancing the Art & Science of Teaching With Technology* (Magaña & Marzano, 2014)
- *Teacher Evaluation That Makes a Difference: A New Model for Teacher Growth and Student Achievement* (Marzano & Toth, 2013)
- *Coaching Classroom Instruction* (Marzano & Simms, 2013a)
- *Becoming a Reflective Teacher* (Marzano, 2012a)
- *Effective Supervision: Supporting the Art and Science of Teaching* (Marzano et al., 2011)
- *The Highly Engaged Classroom* (Marzano & Pickering, 2011)
- *Formative Assessment and Standards-Based Grading* (Marzano, 2010a)
- *On Excellence in Teaching* (Marzano, 2010b)
- *Designing and Teaching Learning Goals and Objectives* (Marzano, 2009)
- *The Art and Science of Teaching: A Comprehensive Framework for Effective Instruction* (Marzano, 2007)
- *Classroom Management That Works: Research-Based Strategies for Every Teacher* (Marzano, 2003a)
- *What Works in Schools: Translating Research Into Action* (Marzano, 2003b)
- *Classroom Instruction That Works: Research-Based Strategies for Increasing Student Achievement* (Marzano, Pickering, & Pollock, 2001)
- *A Different Kind of Classroom: Teaching With Dimensions of Learning* (Marzano, 1992)
- *Dimensions of Thinking: A Framework for Curriculum and Instruction* (Marzano et al., 1988)

Other resources related to an evaluation system focused on development (the critical commitment for level 2), a schoolwide model of instruction, support of teacher growth, professional development, observation and discussion of effective teaching, and other level 2 topics can also be used.

Chapter 3
Guaranteed and Viable Curriculum

• • •

At level 3, school leaders ensure that a guaranteed and viable curriculum (DuFour & Marzano, 2011; Marzano, 2003b) focused on enhancing student learning is in place. *Guaranteed* means that all teachers are aware of the content they are responsible for teaching and are, in fact, teaching that content (usually stated as standards). This approach ensures that every student has the opportunity to learn the grade- and subject-appropriate content on which they will be assessed. *Viable* means that the amount of content is teachable in the time available for instruction. Essentially, a guaranteed and viable curriculum is one that can be taught in the time available and is being taught in every classroom. Level 3 has six leading indicators:

3.1 The school curriculum and accompanying assessments adhere to state and district standards.

3.2 The school curriculum is focused enough that it can be adequately addressed in the time available to teachers.

3.3 All students have the opportunity to learn the critical content of the curriculum.

3.4 Clear and measurable goals are established and focused on critical needs regarding improving overall student achievement at the school level.

3.5 Data are analyzed, interpreted, and used to regularly monitor progress toward school achievement goals.

3.6 Appropriate school- and classroom-level programs and practices are in place to help students meet individual achievement goals when data indicate interventions are needed.

The leading indicators are designed to provide direction for school leaders as they seek to achieve high reliability status for level 3. As at levels 1 and 2, one of the best ways for school leaders to identify areas of strength and weakness in their schools is to use a leading indicator survey.

Level 3 Short-Form Leading Indicator Survey

Figure 3.1 (page 58) presents a short-form leading indicator survey for level 3. This survey can be administered to faculty, staff, and administrators within a school.

1: Strongly disagree	2: Disagree	3: Neither disagree nor agree
4: Agree	5: Strongly agree	N: N/A or don't know

	1	2	3	4	5	N
3.1 The school curriculum and accompanying assessments adhere to state and district standards.	1	2	3	4	5	N
3.2 The school curriculum is focused enough that it can be adequately addressed in the time available to teachers.	1	2	3	4	5	N
3.3 All students have the opportunity to learn the critical content of the curriculum.	1	2	3	4	5	N
3.4 Clear and measurable goals are established and focused on critical needs regarding improving overall student achievement at the school level.	1	2	3	4	5	N
3.5 Data are analyzed, interpreted, and used to regularly monitor progress toward school achievement goals.	1	2	3	4	5	N
3.6 Appropriate school- and classroom-level programs and practices are in place to help students meet individual achievement goals when data indicate interventions are needed.	1	2	3	4	5	N

Figure 3.1: Level 3 short-form leading indicator survey.

This survey provides very general information about a school's level 3 status. For more specific information, long-form surveys should be used.

Level 3 Long-Form Leading Indicator Surveys

The long-form leading indicator surveys are designed to gather specific data about a school's level 3 strengths and weaknesses. School leaders should feel free to adapt the surveys in reproducibles 3.1–3.4 (pages 59–68).

Reproducible 3.1: Level 3 Long-Form Leading Indicator Survey for Teachers and Staff

1: Strongly disagree	2: Disagree	3: Neither disagree nor agree
4: Agree	5: Strongly agree	N: N/A or don't know

3.1 The school curriculum and accompanying assessments adhere to state and district standards.	Our school's written curriculum has been analyzed to ensure that it correlates with state and district standards (for example, the Common Core State Standards [CCSS]).	1	2	3	4	5	N
	Our school's curriculum adequately addresses important 21st century skills (for example, college and career readiness anchor standards and Mathematical Practices from the CCSS).	1	2	3	4	5	N
	Our school's taught curriculum (that is, what is taught in classrooms) has been analyzed to ensure that it correlates with the written curriculum.	1	2	3	4	5	N
	Our school's assessments have been analyzed to ensure that they accurately measure the written and taught curriculum.	1	2	3	4	5	N
	School teams meet regularly to analyze the relationship between our school's written curriculum, our school's taught curriculum, and our school's assessments.	1	2	3	4	5	N
	I can describe the essential content and standards for the subject areas and grade levels that I teach.	1	2	3	4	5	N
3.2 The school curriculum is focused enough that it can be adequately addressed in the time available to teachers.	The essential elements of the content taught in our school have been identified.	1	2	3	4	5	N
	The amount of time needed to adequately address the essential elements of the content taught in our school has been examined.	1	2	3	4	5	N
	School teams meet regularly to discuss and revise (as necessary) documents that articulate essential content and the time needed to teach that content (for example, pacing guides and curriculum maps).	1	2	3	4	5	N
	Essential vocabulary has been identified for Tiers 1, 2, and 3.	1	2	3	4	5	N
3.3 All students have the opportunity to learn the critical content of the curriculum.	Tracking systems at our school are used to examine each student's access to the essential elements of the curriculum.	1	2	3	4	5	N
	Parents at our school are aware of their child's current access to the essential elements of the curriculum.	1	2	3	4	5	N
	All students at our school have access to advanced placement courses.	1	2	3	4	5	N
	The extent to which all students have access to necessary courses has been analyzed.	1	2	3	4	5	N
	I have completed appropriate content training in my subject-area courses.	1	2	3	4	5	N
	Direct vocabulary instruction for Tier 1 terms is provided to those students who need it.	1	2	3	4	5	N
	Direct vocabulary instruction for Tier 2 terms is provided to all students as a regular part of English language arts instruction.	1	2	3	4	5	N
	Direct vocabulary instruction for Tier 3 terms is provided in all subject-area classes.	1	2	3	4	5	N

page 1 of 3

3.4 Clear and measurable goals are established and focused on critical needs regarding improving overall student achievement at the school level.	Our school has set goals regarding the percentage of students who will score at a proficient or higher level on state assessments or benchmark assessments.	1	2	3	4	5	N
	Our school has set goals to eliminate the achievement gap for all students.	1	2	3	4	5	N
	Our school has set goals to eliminate differences in achievement for students at various socioeconomic levels.	1	2	3	4	5	N
	Our school has set goals to eliminate differences in achievement for students of various ethnicities.	1	2	3	4	5	N
	Our school has set goals to eliminate differences in achievement for English learners.	1	2	3	4	5	N
	Our school has set goals to eliminate differences in achievement for students with special needs.	1	2	3	4	5	N
	Our school's goals for student achievement are posted where teachers see them regularly.	1	2	3	4	5	N
	Our school's goals for student achievement are discussed regularly at faculty meetings.	1	2	3	4	5	N
	I can explain how our school's goals eliminate differences in achievement for students at various socioeconomic levels.	1	2	3	4	5	N
	I can explain how our school's goals eliminate differences in achievement for students of various ethnicities.	1	2	3	4	5	N
	I can explain how our school's goals eliminate differences in achievement for English learners.	1	2	3	4	5	N
	I can explain how our school's goals eliminate differences in achievement for students with special needs.	1	2	3	4	5	N
	Various departments and faculty members are responsible for specific improvement goals.	1	2	3	4	5	N
	Our school's goals address our school's most critical and severe deficiencies.	1	2	3	4	5	N
3.5 Data are analyzed, interpreted, and used to regularly monitor progress toward school achievement goals.	Overall student achievement is analyzed regularly at our school.	1	2	3	4	5	N
	Student achievement data are regularly examined from a value-added results perspective.	1	2	3	4	5	N
	We regularly report and use results from multiple types of assessments (for example, benchmark assessments and common assessments).	1	2	3	4	5	N
	I can describe the different types of student data reports available to me.	1	2	3	4	5	N
	Student data reports (including graphs and charts) are updated regularly to track growth in student achievement.	1	2	3	4	5	N
	Our school's leadership team regularly analyzes student growth data.	1	2	3	4	5	N
	Data briefings are conducted regularly at faculty meetings.	1	2	3	4	5	N

3.6 Appropriate school- and classroom-level programs and practices are in place to help students meet individual achievement goals when data indicate interventions are needed.	Our school has extended school day programs in place.	1	2	3	4	5	N
	Our school has extended school week programs in place.	1	2	3	4	5	N
	Our school has extended school year programs in place.	1	2	3	4	5	N
	Our school has after-school programs in place.	1	2	3	4	5	N
	Our school has tutorial programs in place.	1	2	3	4	5	N
	Our school schedule is designed to allow students to receive academic help while in school.	1	2	3	4	5	N
	Students' completion of programs designed to improve their academic achievement (such as gifted and talented education; advanced placement; and science, technology, engineering, and mathematics [STEM]) is monitored.	1	2	3	4	5	N
	Our school has response to intervention measures and programs in place.	1	2	3	4	5	N
	Our school has enrichment programs in place.	1	2	3	4	5	N

Reproducible 3.2: Level 3 Long-Form Leading Indicator Survey for Administrators

1: Strongly disagree	2: Disagree	3: Neither disagree nor agree
4: Agree	5: Strongly agree	N: N/A or don't know

3.1 The school curriculum and accompanying assessments adhere to state and district standards.	Our school's written curriculum has been analyzed to ensure that it correlates with state and district standards (for example, the Common Core State Standards [CCSS]).	1	2	3	4	5	N
	Our school's curriculum adequately addresses important 21st century skills (for example, college and career readiness anchor standards and Mathematical Practices from the CCSS).	1	2	3	4	5	N
	Our school's taught curriculum (that is, what is taught in classrooms) has been analyzed to ensure that it correlates with the written curriculum.	1	2	3	4	5	N
	Our school's assessments have been analyzed to ensure that they accurately measure the written and taught curriculum.	1	2	3	4	5	N
	School teams meet regularly to analyze the relationship between our school's written curriculum, our school's taught curriculum, and our school's assessments.	1	2	3	4	5	N
	Teachers can describe the essential content and standards for the subject areas and grade levels that they teach.	1	2	3	4	5	N
3.2 The school curriculum is focused enough that it can be adequately addressed in the time available to teachers.	The essential elements of the content taught in our school have been identified.	1	2	3	4	5	N
	The amount of time needed to adequately address the essential elements of the content taught in our school has been examined.	1	2	3	4	5	N
	School teams meet regularly to discuss and revise (as necessary) documents that articulate essential content and the time needed to teach that content (for example, pacing guides and curriculum maps).	1	2	3	4	5	N
	Essential vocabulary has been identified for Tiers 1, 2, and 3.	1	2	3	4	5	N
3.3 All students have the opportunity to learn the critical content of the curriculum.	Tracking systems at our school are used to examine each student's access to the essential elements of the curriculum.	1	2	3	4	5	N
	Parents at our school are aware of their child's current access to the essential elements of the curriculum.	1	2	3	4	5	N
	All students at our school have access to advanced placement courses.	1	2	3	4	5	N
	The extent to which all students have access to necessary courses has been analyzed.	1	2	3	4	5	N
	I ensure that teachers have completed appropriate content training in their subject-area courses.	1	2	3	4	5	N
	Direct vocabulary instruction for Tier 1 terms is provided to those students who need it.	1	2	3	4	5	N
	Direct vocabulary instruction for Tier 2 terms is provided to all students as a regular part of English language arts instruction.	1	2	3	4	5	N
	Direct vocabulary instruction for Tier 3 terms is provided in all subject-area classes.	1	2	3	4	5	N

page 1 of 3

3.4 Clear and measurable goals are established and focused on critical needs regarding improving overall student achievement at the school level.	Our school has set goals regarding the percentage of students who will score at a proficient or higher level on state assessments or benchmark assessments.	1	2	3	4	5	N
	Our school has set goals to eliminate the achievement gap for all students.	1	2	3	4	5	N
	Our school has set goals to eliminate differences in achievement for students at various socioeconomic levels.	1	2	3	4	5	N
	Our school has set goals to eliminate differences in achievement for students of various ethnicities.	1	2	3	4	5	N
	Our school has set goals to eliminate differences in achievement for English learners.	1	2	3	4	5	N
	Our school has set goals to eliminate differences in achievement for students with special needs.	1	2	3	4	5	N
	Our school's goals for student achievement are posted where teachers see them regularly.	1	2	3	4	5	N
	Our school's goals for student achievement are discussed regularly at faculty meetings.	1	2	3	4	5	N
	I can explain how our school's goals eliminate differences in achievement for students at various socioeconomic levels.	1	2	3	4	5	N
	I can explain how our school's goals eliminate differences in achievement for students of various ethnicities.	1	2	3	4	5	N
	I can explain how our school's goals eliminate differences in achievement for English learners.	1	2	3	4	5	N
	I can explain how our school's goals eliminate differences in achievement for students with special needs.	1	2	3	4	5	N
	Various departments and faculty members are responsible for specific improvement goals.	1	2	3	4	5	N
	Our school's goals address our school's most critical and severe deficiencies.	1	2	3	4	5	N
3.5 Data are analyzed, interpreted, and used to regularly monitor progress toward school achievement goals.	Overall student achievement is analyzed regularly at our school.	1	2	3	4	5	N
	Student achievement data are regularly examined from a value-added results perspective.	1	2	3	4	5	N
	Teachers at our school regularly report and use results from multiple types of assessments (for example, benchmark assessments and common assessments).	1	2	3	4	5	N
	Teachers at our school can describe the different types of student data reports available to them.	1	2	3	4	5	N
	Student data reports (including graphs and charts) are updated regularly to track growth in student achievement.	1	2	3	4	5	N
	Our school's leadership team regularly analyzes student growth data.	1	2	3	4	5	N
	Data briefings are conducted regularly at faculty meetings.	1	2	3	4	5	N

3.6 Appropriate school- and classroom-level programs and practices are in place to help students meet individual achievement goals when data indicate interventions are needed.	Our school has extended school day programs in place.	1	2	3	4	5	N
	Our school has extended school week programs in place.	1	2	3	4	5	N
	Our school has extended school year programs in place.	1	2	3	4	5	N
	Our school has after-school programs in place.	1	2	3	4	5	N
	Our school has tutorial programs in place.	1	2	3	4	5	N
	Our school schedule is designed to allow students to receive academic help while in school.	1	2	3	4	5	N
	Students' completion of programs designed to improve their academic achievement (such as gifted and talented education; advanced placement; and science, technology, engineering, and mathematics [STEM]) is monitored.	1	2	3	4	5	N
	Our school has response to intervention measures and programs in place.	1	2	3	4	5	N
	Our school has enrichment programs in place.	1	2	3	4	5	N

Reproducible 3.3: Level 3 Long-Form Leading Indicator Survey for Students

| 1: Strongly disagree | 2: Disagree | 3: Neither disagree nor agree |
| 4: Agree | 5: Strongly agree | N: N/A or don't know |

3.1 The school curriculum and accompanying assessments adhere to state and district standards.	In school, I learn skills that will help me succeed in college or in a career.	1	2	3	4	5	N
	The exams, quizzes, and tests that I take in school are about information and skills that my teachers have taught.	1	2	3	4	5	N
	My teachers meet with each other regularly to discuss how well students are learning.	1	2	3	4	5	N
	My teachers know the information they need to know to teach the classes they teach.	1	2	3	4	5	N
3.2 The school curriculum is focused enough that it can be adequately addressed in the time available to teachers.	My teachers are able to teach what they need to teach in the time available.	1	2	3	4	5	N
	My teachers meet with each other regularly to discuss what they are teaching.	1	2	3	4	5	N
	There are specific vocabulary words that I need to learn in each of my classes.	1	2	3	4	5	N
3.3 All students have the opportunity to learn the critical content of the curriculum.	I am taught everything that I need to learn.	1	2	3	4	5	N
	My parents know what I am being taught.	1	2	3	4	5	N
	I can take advanced placement courses if I want to.	1	2	3	4	5	N
	My teachers check to make sure that I am being taught everything I need to learn.	1	2	3	4	5	N
	My teachers take classes to learn more about the subjects they teach.	1	2	3	4	5	N
	If English is not my first language, I am taught basic English words that I need to know.	1	2	3	4	5	N
	In English language arts, I learn about academic words I need to know to read advanced texts.	1	2	3	4	5	N
	In my subject-area classes, I learn about vocabulary words I need to know to understand information about each subject.	1	2	3	4	5	N
3.4 Clear and measurable goals are established and focused on critical needs regarding improving overall student achievement at the school level.	Most of the students at our school score well on exams, quizzes, and tests.	1	2	3	4	5	N
	I score well on exams, quizzes, and tests.	1	2	3	4	5	N

page 1 of 2

3.5 Data are analyzed, interpreted, and used to regularly monitor progress toward school achievement goals.	My teachers and our school's leaders know how well I am doing in school.	1	2	3	4	5	N
	My teachers collect and talk about my scores on exams, quizzes, and tests.	1	2	3	4	5	N
	My teachers have reports that show how well I am doing in class.	1	2	3	4	5	N
	My teachers talk about how I am doing in class when they meet together.	1	2	3	4	5	N
3.6 Appropriate school- and classroom-level programs and practices are in place to help students meet individual achievement goals when data indicate interventions are needed.	My school has programs that extend the school day.	1	2	3	4	5	N
	My school has programs that extend the school week.	1	2	3	4	5	N
	My school has programs that extend the school year.	1	2	3	4	5	N
	My school has after-school programs available.	1	2	3	4	5	N
	My school has tutorial programs available.	1	2	3	4	5	N
	My school has enrichment programs available.	1	2	3	4	5	N
	I can get academic help during school hours if I need it.	1	2	3	4	5	N
	My school keeps track of my participation in and completion of programs that help me extend my learning (such as gifted and talented education; advanced placement; and science, technology, engineering, and mathematics [STEM]).	1	2	3	4	5	N
	If I am having trouble learning, someone in my school does something to help me learn.	1	2	3	4	5	N

Reproducible 3.4: Level 3 Long-Form Leading Indicator Survey for Parents

1: Strongly disagree	2: Disagree	3: Neither disagree nor agree
4: Agree	5: Strongly agree	N: N/A or don't know

3.1 The school curriculum and accompanying assessments adhere to state and district standards.	The curriculum at my child's school is aligned to state and district standards (for example, the Common Core State Standards [CCSS]).	1	2	3	4	5	N
	The curriculum at my child's school adequately addresses important 21st century skills to prepare students for college and careers.	1	2	3	4	5	N
	The content taught by teachers at my child's school matches the content articulated in the school's curriculum documents.	1	2	3	4	5	N
	The exams, quizzes, and tests at my child's school accurately measure the content taught by teachers and articulated in the school's curriculum documents.	1	2	3	4	5	N
	Teachers at my child's school are knowledgeable about the subject areas they teach.	1	2	3	4	5	N
3.2 The school curriculum is focused enough that it can be adequately addressed in the time available to teachers.	Teachers at my child's school know what they are supposed to teach.	1	2	3	4	5	N
	Teachers at my child's school have enough time to teach what they are supposed to teach.	1	2	3	4	5	N
	The vocabulary terms that my child will learn at school have been clearly specified.	1	2	3	4	5	N
3.3 All students have the opportunity to learn the critical content of the curriculum.	My child has access to the classes he or she needs to learn the essential elements of the curriculum.	1	2	3	4	5	N
	I am aware of my child's current access to the essential elements of the curriculum.	1	2	3	4	5	N
	My child has access to advanced placement courses.	1	2	3	4	5	N
	My child's teachers have completed appropriate content training in their subject-area courses.	1	2	3	4	5	N
	If English is not my child's first language, he or she is taught basic English words necessary for basic communication and comprehension.	1	2	3	4	5	N
	In English language arts, my child learns academic words necessary to read advanced texts.	1	2	3	4	5	N
	In his or her subject-area classes, my child learns vocabulary words necessary to understand subject-specific information.	1	2	3	4	5	N

page | 1 of 2

A Handbook for High Reliability Schools © 2014 Marzano Research • marzanoresearch.com

3.4 Clear and measurable goals are established and focused on critical needs regarding improving overall student achievement at the school level.	Most of the students at my child's school score well on exams, quizzes, and tests.	1	2	3	4	5	N
	My child scores well on exams, quizzes, and tests.	1	2	3	4	5	N
3.5 Data are analyzed, interpreted, and used to regularly monitor progress toward school achievement goals.	Teachers and leaders at my child's school know how well my child is doing in school.	1	2	3	4	5	N
	My child's teachers collect data and discuss my child's performance on exams, quizzes, and tests.	1	2	3	4	5	N
	Teachers at my child's school have reports that show how well my child is doing in class.	1	2	3	4	5	N
	Teachers at my child's school talk about how well my child is doing in class when they meet together.	1	2	3	4	5	N
3.6 Appropriate school- and classroom-level programs and practices are in place to help students meet individual achievement goals when data indicate interventions are needed.	My child's school has extended school day programs in place.	1	2	3	4	5	N
	My child's school has extended school week programs in place.	1	2	3	4	5	N
	My child's school has extended school year programs in place.	1	2	3	4	5	N
	My child's school has after-school programs in place.	1	2	3	4	5	N
	My child's school has tutorial programs in place.	1	2	3	4	5	N
	The schedule at my child's school is designed to allow students to receive academic help while in school.	1	2	3	4	5	N
	My child's school keeps track of my child's participation in and completion of programs designed to improve his or her academic achievement (such as gifted and talented education; advanced placement; and science, technology, engineering, and mathematics [STEM]).	1	2	3	4	5	N
	My child's school has response to intervention measures and programs in place.	1	2	3	4	5	N
	My child's school has enrichment programs in place.	1	2	3	4	5	N

As at levels 1 and 2, teachers, staff, administrators, students, and parents complete the appropriate level 3 surveys from reproducibles 3.1–3.4, and school leaders identify areas of strength (to be documented using lagging indicators) and weakness (to be addressed through critical commitments and monitored using lagging indicators). For example, school leaders observe that faculty members rated leading indicator 3.3, "All students have the opportunity to learn the critical content of the curriculum," particularly low. Upon investigation, the leaders find that teachers feel the school's English learners do not have equal opportunities to learn the content of the school's curriculum because of their limited vocabulary proficiency. As a result, they implement a program of direct vocabulary instruction, one of the critical commitments for level 3.

Level 3 Critical Commitments

The bedrock for level 3 high reliability status is a guaranteed and viable curriculum. The concept of a guaranteed and viable curriculum was addressed in the book *What Works in Schools* (Marzano, 2003b). Although the phrase was first coined in that book, research had been accumulating for years supporting its importance. Perhaps the most relevant studies are those regarding opportunity to learn (OTL). The concept of OTL was introduced by the International Association for the Evaluation of Educational Achievement (see Wilkins, 1997) when it became a component of the First and then, later, the Second International Mathematics Study (FIMS and SIMS, respectively) (see Burstein, 1992; Husén, 1967a, 1967b).

The logic behind OTL is that all students should have equal opportunities to learn the content of the items being used to assess their achievement:

> One of the factors which may influence scores on an achievement examination is whether or not the students have had an opportunity to study a particular topic or learn how to solve a particular type of problem presented by the test. (Husén, 1967b, pp. 162–163)

OTL is a very simple concept—if students do not have the opportunity to learn the content expected of them, there is, of course, little chance that they will. As it relates to level 3 high reliability status, OTL addresses the extent to which the curriculum in a school is *guaranteed*. Operationally, this means that the curriculum provides clear guidance regarding the content to be addressed in specific courses and at specific grade levels. Additionally, it means that individual teachers do not have the option to disregard or replace content that has been designated as essential to a specific course or grade level. This constitutes the guaranteed part of a guaranteed and viable curriculum.

The criterion of viability is equally important and is, in fact, a necessary condition for having a guaranteed curriculum. Viability means that the content teachers are expected to address can be adequately addressed in the time teachers have available for instruction. Unfortunately, for years, K–12 education has ignored the problem of too much content in its standards. Marzano, Yanoski, Hoegh, and Simms (2013) commented on the proliferation of content that resulted from the standards movement of the 1990s: "As different subject-matter organizations developed standards for their specific content areas, each group of specialists identified *everything* they thought students should know and be able to do in their fields" (p. 2). As a result, the standards developed by subject-matter organizations during the 1990s presented far too much content for teachers to address. Stated differently, the curriculum recommended or implied by the standards initiatives of the 1990s was, by definition, not viable and therefore could not be guaranteed.

The Common Core State Standards Initiative sought to alleviate the problem of too much content in previous standards efforts:

> The National Governors Association (NGA) and the Council of Chief State School Officers (CCSSO) met in 2009 and agreed to take part in "a state-led process that will draw on evidence and lead to development

and adoption of a common core of state standards . . . in English language arts and mathematics for grades K–12" (as cited in Rothman, 2011, p. 62). Other organizations also contributed to the effort, among them Achieve, the Alliance for Excellent Education, the James B. Hunt Jr. Institute for Educational Leadership and Policy, the National Association of State Boards of Education, the Business Roundtable, ACT, and the College Board (Rothman, 2011). These organizations created a set of three criteria that would guide the design of the CCSS. (Marzano et al., 2013, p. 6)

One of the three criteria established was that "the new standards should be fewer, clearer, and higher than previous standards. That is, there should be *fewer* standards statements, they should be *clearer* (unidimensional and concrete), and they should encourage students to use *higher*-level thinking" (Marzano et al., 2013, p. 6). While the CCSS effort did succeed in reducing the amount of content in mathematics and English language arts, not all agreed that the new standards were completely viable and useful to K–12 schools (for a discussion, see Marzano et al., 2013).

In addition to a curriculum that is guaranteed and viable, level 3 status requires a curriculum that enhances student learning. This means that in addition to traditional content, the curriculum also addresses skills that help students learn. This emphasis is explicit in the CCSS, particularly in the Standards for Mathematical Practice and the college and career readiness anchor standards in English language arts. Marzano and his colleagues (2013) noted that these standards involve "mental processes that could be directly taught to students and then used to apply mathematics and ELA content in meaningful ways" (p. 23). Many of these standards represent metacognitive skills. Level 3 high reliability status, then, requires significant tightening and focus in the school curriculum and how it is used by teachers.

Level 3 has three critical commitments associated with it: (1) continually monitor the viability of the curriculum, (2) create a comprehensive vocabulary program, and (3) use direct instruction in knowledge application and metacognitive skills.

Continually Monitor the Viability of the Curriculum

Given the focus of level 3, an obvious and necessary initiative is continually monitoring the viability of the curriculum with respect to the amount of time available for instruction. In fact, this should probably be the starting place for any school that seeks level 3 high reliability status. Two approaches to such an audit are discussed in the book *What Works in Schools* (Marzano, 2003b). One involves asking teachers to estimate the number of hours it would take to address the essential content within the curriculum and then comparing the total hours from this estimate with the hours available for instruction. The second involves asking teachers to estimate the number of class periods it would take to address the essential content and then comparing this total with the class periods available. These simple actions done continually will help a school avoid the pitfall of taking on too many new programs that include new content.

Create a Comprehensive Vocabulary Program

Taken at face value, it might seem that a comprehensive vocabulary program is not a critical aspect of a guaranteed and viable curriculum that enhances student learning. However, both research and common sense indicate that vocabulary development is critical to enhancing student learning. Stated differently, vocabulary knowledge is so foundational to content knowledge that it should be a focal point of the curriculum.

Numerous studies have documented the relationship between vocabulary knowledge and academic achievement:

Students' vocabulary knowledge is directly tied to their success in school. This is partly because vocabulary is an important aspect of reading comprehension (Cunningham & Stanovich, 1997; Hattie, 2009; National Reading Panel, 2000; Petty, Herold, & Stoll, 1967; Scarborough, 2001; Stahl, 1999; Stahl & Nagy, 2006) and reading is an important part of learning in school. However, vocabulary knowledge helps students in other ways as well. Knowing what words mean and how they interconnect creates networks of knowledge that allow students to connect new information to previously learned information. These networks of knowledge are commonly referred to as *prior knowledge* or *background knowledge* (Marzano, 2004). Studies have shown that students with greater background knowledge about a topic learn more, remember more, and are more interested when that topic is taught than those who have less initial background knowledge (Alexander, Kulikowich, & Schulze, 1994; Dochy, Segers, & Buehl, 1999; Tobias, 1994). (Marzano & Simms, 2013b, p. 5)

A question that immediately surfaces in any discussion of vocabulary instruction is, Which vocabulary terms should be the subject of direct instruction? Certainly, not all terms students encounter should be taught directly. There are a variety of perspectives on this issue, and some have proposed that formally identifying vocabulary that will be taught directly is so problematic as to be not worth the effort (for a discussion, see Marzano, 2004, 2010c). Fortunately, viable solutions have been proposed.

Isabel Beck and Margaret McKeown (1985) explained that vocabulary terms can be thought of in three tiers. The first tier includes those terms that are very frequent in the English language—the most basic terms in the language that are encountered frequently enough that students commonly learn them in context. Tier 2 terms are those that are important to understanding a language but appear infrequently enough in general language usage that they will probably not be learned from context. Tier 3 terms in the Beck and McKeown schema are subject-matter specific—terms that are important to academic subject areas but not as frequently found in general use in the language.

Tier 1 and Tier 2 Terms

In the book *Teaching Basic and Advanced Vocabulary*, Marzano (2010c) identified 2,845 Tier 1 terms and 5,162 Tier 2 terms and, for ease of instruction, organized those Tier 1 and Tier 2 terms into groups of related terms called *semantic clusters*. For example, table 3.1 shows the Tier 1 and some of the Tier 2 terms from a semantic cluster titled "Bodies of Water."

Table 3.1: Tier 1 and Tier 2 Terms in the Semantic Cluster "Bodies of Water"

Tier 1	Tier 2
ocean	brook
puddle	cove
river	strait
sea	swamp
stream	tributary
bay	lagoon
creek	
pond	

The advantage to organizing terms in semantic clusters is that multiple words can be taught simultaneously. Additionally, students will typically already know at least some of the words in a cluster, which will serve as an anchor for learning the other words. For example, assume students are generally aware of the Tier 1 term *ocean*. This provides a foundation for learning the Tier 1 term *sea*. During the same lesson in which *sea* is introduced, the teacher also elects to introduce the Tier 1 term *bay* and the Tier 2 term *cove* because of their close relationship to each other and their more distant but still important relationship to the terms *ocean* and *sea*. In effect, the semantic clusters provide an effective way to teach Tier 1 terms and Tier 2 terms in a rich, semantically similar environment.

It is important to note that not all Tier 1 and Tier 2 terms have to be taught. This would be inefficient. While the vast majority of the 2,845 Tier 1 terms can be taught fairly efficiently, the 5,162 Tier 2 terms are too numerous to address efficiently through direct instruction. Thus, a school should carefully select the Tier 2 terms that are important enough to its curriculum to be taught directly. One group of Tier 2 terms commonly selected for direct instruction is cognitive verbs—terms that represent the mental operations students are required to execute when interacting with complex content like that identified in the CCSS. Table 3.2 reports 227 Tier 2 cognitive verbs, again organized in semantic clusters.

Table 3.2: Tier 2 Cognitive Verbs

Semantic Cluster	Terms
Add To	combine, deepen, improve, incorporate, integrate, introduce
Arrange	arrange, list, organize, sort
Collaborate	collaborate, contribute, engage, interact, participate, share
Compare/ Contrast	associate, categorize, classify, compare, connect, contrast, differentiate, discriminate, distinguish, link, match, relate
Create	accomplish, achieve, build, compose, construct, create, develop, draft, form, generate, initiate, produce, publish, record, stimulate
Decide	choose, decide, select
Define	define, delineate, determine, discern, establish, exemplify, identify, interpret, label, locate, name, recall, recognize
Elaborate	broaden, derive, elaborate, enhance, expand
Evaluate	assess, check, critique, evaluate, judge
Execute	advance, calculate, compute, conduct, employ, execute, navigate
Explain	answer, articulate, clarify, communicate, convey, describe, explain, express, inform, narrate, present, recount, report, respond, retell, state, summarize, synthesize
Hypothesize	anticipate, approximate, conjecture, consider, estimate, experiment, explore, hypothesize, pose, predict, test
Infer	conclude, deduce, generalize, infer, reason
Measure	gauge, measure, quantify
Problem Solve	figure out, overcome, problem solve, resolve, solve, surmount
Prove/Argue	argue, assert, challenge, claim, confirm, defend, disagree, justify, persuade, promote, prove, qualify, specify, support, verify
Pull Apart	analyze, decompose, decontextualize, diagnose, examine, grapple, investigate, partition, probe

Redo	redo, repeat, reread, revisit
Reference	acknowledge, cite, consult, plagiarize, refer, reference, trace
Seek Information	acquire, ask, capture, compile, detect, elicit, encounter, evoke, find out, gather, listen, note, notice, observe, question, request, research, search, seek, study
See the Big Picture	comprehend, contextualize, orient, understand
Symbolize	act out, chart, conceptualize, demonstrate, depict, diagram, graph, illustrate, imagine, map, model, represent, symbolize, visualize
Think Metacognitively	appreciate, attend, design, monitor, persevere, plan, prepare, reflect, self-correct
Transform	accentuate, adapt, adjust, alter, apply, conform, convert, edit, emphasize, manipulate, modify, paraphrase, rearrange, refine, replace, revise, rewrite, shape, shift, simplify, strengthen, substitute, tailor, transform, translate, update

Source: Adapted from Marzano & Simms, 2013b.

Tier 3 Domain-Specific Terms

In *Building Background Knowledge for Academic Achievement*, Marzano (2004) identified 7,923 Tier 3 domain-specific terms. The numbers of Tier 3 terms for various subject areas are reported in table 3.3 (page 74). When these Tier 3 terms are added to the 2,845 Tier 1 terms and 5,162 Tier 2 terms, the total is 15,930. However, some 900 terms can be found in more than one tier. This brings the total down to approximately 15,000 terms. In effect, schools now have a corpus of 15,000 terms that can be used to develop the foundational vocabulary knowledge for any student at any level in any subject area.

A reasonable approach to direct vocabulary instruction would have the following characteristics:

- Direct instruction in the Tier 1 terms only for those students who need it
- Direct instruction in the Tier 2 terms for all students as a regular part of instruction in the English language arts
- Direct instruction in Tier 3 terms as part of instruction in subject-area classes

Such an approach allows all students to learn the terms that they need to be successful in school and provides additional vocabulary support to non-native speakers who may need direct instruction in Tier 1 terms.

Use Direct Instruction in Knowledge Application and Metacognitive Skills

As described previously, the CCSS place an emphasis on explicit instruction in knowledge application and metacognitive skills. This emphasis is not new or unique to the CCSS. Over the past few decades, mental processes that could be used to apply content in meaningful ways have been called by many other names, such as thinking and reasoning skills (Marzano & Pollock, 2001), habits of mind (Costa & Kallick, 2009), learning and innovation skills (Partnership for 21st Century Skills, 2012), workplace demands (U.S. Department of Labor, Secretary's Commission on Achieving Necessary Skills, 1991), dimensions of learning (Marzano & Pickering, 1997), dimensions of thinking (Marzano et al., 1988), and transferable knowledge (Pellegrino & Hilton, 2012), among others.

Table 3.3: Tier 3 Terms in Seventeen Subject Areas

Subject Area	(K–2)	(3–5)	(6–8)	(9–12)	Totals
Mathematics	80	190	201	214	685
Science	100	166	225	282	773
English Language Arts	83	245	247	223	798
History					
General History	162	560	319	270	1,311
U.S. History	0	154	123	148	425
World History	0	245	301	297	843
Geography	89	212	258	300	859
Civics	45	145	210	213	613
Economics	29	68	89	155	341
Health	60	68	75	77	280
Physical Education	57	100	50	34	241
The Arts					
Arts General	14	36	30	9	89
Dance	18	24	42	37	121
Music	14	83	67	32	196
Theater	5	14	35	13	67
Visual Arts	3	41	24	8	76
Technology	23	47	56	79	205
Totals	782	2,398	2,352	2,391	7,923

Source: Marzano, 2004, p. 115.

Knowledge application and metacognitive skills can be organized into two broad categories of skills: (1) cognitive and (2) conative. *Cognitive skills* are those needed to effectively process information and complete tasks. *Conative skills* allow a person to examine his or her knowledge and emotions in order to choose an appropriate future course of action. There are ten cognitive skills and seven conative skills that have considerable research behind their efficacy and should be the subject of explicit instruction within the guaranteed and viable curriculum. Each skill is briefly described in table 3.4.

The three critical commitments described here provide a strong foundation for addressing the six leading indicators for level 3. Continually monitoring the viability of the curriculum directly addresses leading indicator 3.2 and provides a foundation for addressing leading indicators 3.1, 3.3, and 3.5. A comprehensive vocabulary program and explicit instruction in knowledge application and metacognitive skills facilitate leading indicators 3.4 and 3.6.

Table 3.4: Cognitive and Conative Skills

Cognitive Skills	Conative Skills
Generating conclusions involves combining known information to form new ideas.	**Becoming aware of the power of interpretations** involves becoming aware that one's thoughts, feelings, beliefs, and actions are influenced by how one interprets situations.
Identifying common logical errors involves analyzing information to determine how true it is.	**Cultivating a growth mindset** involves building the belief that each person can increase his or her intelligence and abilities.
Presenting and supporting claims involves providing evidence to support a new idea.	**Cultivating resiliency** involves developing the ability to overcome failure, challenges, or adversity.
Navigating digital sources involves using electronic resources to find credible and relevant information.	**Avoiding negative thinking** involves preventing one's emotions from dictating one's thoughts and actions.
Problem solving involves accomplishing a goal in spite of obstacles or limiting conditions.	**Taking various perspectives** involves identifying the reasoning behind multiple (and often conflicting) perspectives on an issue.
Decision making involves using criteria to select among alternatives that initially appear to be equal.	**Interacting responsibly** involves being accountable for the outcome of an interaction.
Experimenting is the process of generating and testing explanations of observed phenomena.	**Handling controversy and conflict resolution** involves reacting positively to controversy or conflict.
Investigating involves identifying confusions or contradictions about ideas or events and suggesting ways to resolve those confusions or contradictions.	
Identifying basic relationships between ideas involves consciously analyzing how one idea relates to others.	
Generating and manipulating mental images involves creating a picture of information in one's mind in order to process it more deeply.	

Source: Adapted from Marzano et al., 2013, pp. 26–44.

Level 3 Lagging Indicators

As with levels 1 and 2, lagging indicators and corresponding criterion scores should be formulated to measure a school's progress toward and achievement of level 3, particularly in areas initially perceived as weak. The following are examples of statements that could be used as lagging indicators for level 3:

- Curriculum documents have been created that correlate the written curriculum to state and district standards (for example, the CCSS, if applicable).

- Curriculum documents have been created that correlate the written curriculum to 21st century skills (for example, college and career readiness anchor standards and Mathematical Practices from the CCSS).

- Data show a very strong positive correlation (90 percent or higher) between what is taught in classrooms (that is, the taught curriculum) and the written curriculum.

- Data show a very strong positive correlation (90 percent or higher) between assessments and the written and taught curricula.

- A written list of essential standards or content in the curriculum is in place.

- A written list of essential vocabulary is in place for all levels (that is, Tiers 1, 2, and 3).

- A curriculum audit document shows that the time it would take to adequately address the essential elements of the curriculum does not exceed the instructional time available.

- Written goals exist and specify the percentage of students who will score at a proficient or higher level on state assessments or benchmark assessments, and progress toward these goals is monitored on a bimonthly basis.

- Written goals exist for eliminating differences in achievement between students at different socioeconomic levels, and progress toward these goals is monitored on a bimonthly basis.

- Written goals exist for eliminating differences in achievement between students of different ethnicities, and progress toward these goals is monitored on a bimonthly basis.

- Written goals exist for eliminating the achievement gap for all students, and progress toward these goals is monitored on a bimonthly basis.

- Written goals exist for eliminating differences in achievement for English learners, and progress toward these goals is monitored on a bimonthly basis.

- Written goals exist for eliminating differences in achievement for students with disabilities, and progress toward these goals is monitored on a bimonthly basis.

- Written reports are produced on a monthly basis describing specific actions that have been taken when goals were not met.

- For each goal, a written timeline is available that lists specific benchmarks for the goal and the individuals responsible for the goal.

- Tracking sheets show that reports, graphs, and charts are regularly updated to show growth in student achievement.

- Documentation is available showing that students who need instructional support outside of the regular classroom have had access to and have taken advantage of such support.

Again, these are only examples of the type of lagging indicators a school might use. While there is no set number of lagging indicators a school should use, information gleaned from leading indicator surveys can identify areas of perceived weakness for which lagging indicators will be developed. Table 3.5 can facilitate the process of moving from leading to lagging indicators. After selecting the leading indicators most relevant to their school and designing lagging indicators and criterion scores for each one, school leaders can implement plans to achieve those lagging indicators and collect data to confirm their progress and success. The following examples illustrate how various school leaders might conduct the process.

Example 1

On the leading indicator survey for level 3, a principal notices that teachers of grades 3–5 give particularly low responses for leading indicator 3.2, "The school curriculum is focused enough that it can be adequately addressed in the time available to teachers." Although these results are not surprising since the district recently adopted new science and social studies standards for grades 3–5, the principal creates a plan to ensure that the curriculum for those grades is teachable in the time available.

First, he works with grade-level teams at grades 3, 4, and 5 to label the new science and social studies standards as *essential, nonessential but good to have*, and *nonessential*. Then, he asks each teacher to estimate how long it will take to teach each essential standard. Finally, he compares teachers' estimates with the instructional time available for science and social studies and works with each group to adjust its lists based on the estimates.

To track progress in this area, he designs a lagging indicator and criterion score: "Curriculum maps exist showing which standards are essential and how long they will take to teach." To meet the lagging indicator, he asks each grade-level team to create a curriculum map showing when and how long each essential standard

Table 3.5: Lagging Indicator Determination Chart for Level 3

Leading Indicators for Level 3	Used as Basis for a Lagging Indicator?	Lagging Indicator(s)	Criterion Score or Concrete Product
3.1 The school curriculum and accompanying assessments adhere to state and district standards.			
3.2 The school curriculum is focused enough that it can be adequately addressed in the time available to teachers.			
3.3 All students have the opportunity to learn the critical content of the curriculum.			
3.4 Clear and measurable goals are established and focused on critical needs regarding improving overall student achievement at the school level.			
3.5 Data are analyzed, interpreted, and used to regularly monitor progress toward school achievement goals.			
3.6 Appropriate school- and classroom-level programs and practices are in place to help students meet individual achievement goals when data indicate interventions are needed.			

Visit **marzanoresearch.com/reproducibles/leadership** *to download a reproducible version of this form.*

will be taught. Although kindergarten, first-, and second-grade teachers didn't initially give low responses to leading indicator 3.2, they appreciate the clarity that identifying essential standards and mapping timeframes brings.

Example 2

A middle school principal expects and receives low staff responses to leading indicator 3.6, "Appropriate school- and classroom-level programs and practices are in place to help students meet individual achievement goals when data indicate interventions are needed," on the level 3 leading indicator survey. The school's large English learner population has been straining the intervention resources of the school, and despite teachers' best efforts, EL students are falling behind in all content areas.

In response to the survey results, the principal decides to implement a schoolwide program of direct vocabulary instruction. Teachers identify the vocabulary terms most critical to the content being taught and begin to teach them explicitly before addressing content. They introduce terms to students by describing them, direct students to write their own descriptions and draw pictures for each term, and then ask students to talk about and play with the words. As students learn more about each word, they revise their descriptions and drawings.

To track the school's progress, the principal designs a lagging indicator and criterion score: "Eighty percent of English learners will score proficient or better on assessments of their knowledge of math and science terms." After a month of direct vocabulary instruction, only 60 percent of ELs score proficient or above. However, after three months, 76 percent of ELs are scoring at the proficient or above level, and after five months, 88 percent of ELs achieve proficient or above on vocabulary tests. To further boost ELs' learning, the principal asks the school's ESL teachers to use the same program of vocabulary instruction to address Tier 1 terms that native speakers already know but that ELs might have trouble with.

Example 3

A high school principal finds that staff responses to the level 3 leading indicator survey are lowest for leading indicator 3.4, "Clear and measurable goals are established and focused on critical needs regarding improving overall student achievement at the school level." He is surprised since he made a point to set goals for each grade level in each content area at the beginning of each year, based on the previous years' state testing data. Taking his goals with him, he meets with the school's leadership team and asks them what they think. Most members of the team indicate that although goals are set each year, they aren't clearly communicated to teachers and aren't talked about until state testing data become available the next year.

The principal realizes he needs to ensure that teachers not only know about the goals but also receive regular feedback on students' progress throughout the year. To accomplish this, the principal organizes a system of benchmark testing. Each content-area team creates a common assessment to be given at the end of each quarter. The principal compiles student scores from the benchmark assessments each quarter and reports the data to teachers, along with whether student achievement is on track, ahead of schedule, or lagging behind where it needs to be to meet the school's goals for the year.

To measure the school's success, he designs a lagging indicator and criterion score: "All students will have three or more benchmark scores recorded each year in each subject area." Using a spreadsheet to track students' scores allows the principal to identify content areas with critical needs and implement interventions to raise students' scores in those areas.

Quick Data for Level 3

Once high reliability status has been achieved for level 3, continual monitoring can be accomplished by using quick data. Here, we provide sample questions and incidents based on the leading indicators for level 3. We also provide suggestions for easy-to-collect quantitative data and ways to acknowledge and celebrate success.

Quick Conversations

Quick conversations for level 3 could include the following questions:

3.1 Recently, to what extent has it been apparent that the school curriculum and its accompanying assessments adhere to state and district standards?

3.2 Recently, to what extent has it been apparent that the school curriculum is focused enough to be adequately addressed in the time available to teachers?

3.3 Recently, to what extent has it been apparent that all students have the opportunity to learn the critical content of the curriculum?

3.4 Recently, to what extent has it been apparent that clear and measurable goals focused on critical needs regarding improving overall student achievement at the school level have been established?

3.5 Recently, to what extent has it been apparent that data have been analyzed, interpreted, and used to regularly monitor progress toward school achievement goals?

3.6 Recently, to what extent has it been apparent that appropriate school- and classroom-level programs and practices are in place to help students meet individual achievement goals when data indicate interventions are needed?

Teachers from collaborative teams might ask one or more of these questions during a given interval of time. Responses would be coded as *excellent*, *adequate*, or *unsatisfactory*. These findings would be summarized, perhaps once per month.

Quick Observations

Additionally, quick observations could be made for level 3 indicators. Such observations should focus on recent incidents that indicate the following:

- The school curriculum and accompanying assessments adhere to state and district standards.
- The school curriculum and accompanying assessments do not adhere to state and district standards.
- The school curriculum is focused enough that it can be adequately addressed in the time available to teachers.
- The school curriculum is not focused enough that it can be adequately addressed in the time available to teachers.
- All students have the opportunity to learn the critical content of the curriculum.
- All students do not have the opportunity to learn the critical content of the curriculum.
- Clear and measurable goals focused on critical needs regarding improving overall student achievement have been established.
- Clear and measurable goals focused on critical needs regarding improving overall student achievement have not been established.
- Data have been analyzed, interpreted, and used to monitor progress toward school achievement goals.
- Data have not been analyzed, interpreted, and used to monitor progress toward school achievement goals.
- Appropriate school- and classroom-level programs and practices are in place to help students meet individual achievement goals when data indicate interventions are needed.
- Appropriate school- and classroom-level programs and practices are not in place to help students meet individual achievement goals when data indicate interventions are needed.

Anecdotal notes can be used to keep track of data gathered from quick observations and then summarized in a short narrative.

Easy-to-Collect Quantitative Data

In addition to quick conversations and quick observations, easy-to-collect level 3 quantitative data can be used to continually monitor level 3 performance. Such data might include:

- Recent curriculum audit reports from the state department of education (school improvement or unified improvement plan reports)

- Recent reports from school curriculum committees

- Teacher, team, school, or district alignment documents for essential learnings and school resources

- Curriculum pacing guides that denote suggested approximate amounts of time for each essential learning

- Course approval request forms that denote alignment to state and national standards

- Evidence that typical pathways students take (advanced, regular, technical, and so on) fulfill essential learning requirements

- School improvement documents or school schedules that denote action plans for all students (math labs for students needing extra time or practice, access time for students to work one-on-one with teachers every week for ninety minutes, and so on)

- Student individualized education plans (IEPs) and individual language plans (ILPs) that show connections to essential learnings and proficiency scales

- Student tracking sheets for progress toward essential learning goals

- Class tracking sheets for progress toward essential learning goals

- Curriculum alignment document with most recent alignment dates

- Reports on obtrusive formative assessment data collected from students using polling technology

Acknowledging and Celebrating Success

Periodically, the quick data gathered for level 3 are reported and celebrated. It is important to note that data from all levels for which high reliability status has been obtained are systematically acknowledged and celebrated, as in the following vignette.

> *Mullins Middle School collects quick data about high reliability levels 1–3 and reports the results to the school community in its monthly newsletter. The Celebrations Column features data from quick conversations and quick observations as well as easy-to-collect quantitative data. This month, members of the school's collaborative teams collect quick data on three indicators: one from level 1, one from level 2, and one from level 3. For each indicator, a question is formulated for quick conversations and incident descriptions are designed for quick observations. For level 1, data collectors ask, "To what extent have teachers, students, and parents had opportunities to provide input into the operations of the school?" For level 2, they ask, "To what extent are teachers provided with job-embedded professional development that is directly related to their instructional growth goals?" Finally, for level 3, members of the school community are asked, "To what extent do all students have the opportunity to learn the critical content of the curriculum?" The Celebrations Column features a bar graph for each question showing the school's results (figure 3.2).*

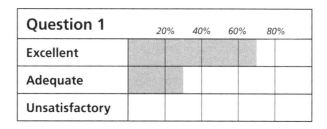

Figure 3.2: Celebrations Column bar graph.

> *Accompanying each question graph is a short narrative describing specific incidents that show the school is meeting expectations for those indicators. In cases where incidents have occurred that show the school is not meeting expectations, or for graphs (like the one for question 3) where some responses were coded unsatisfactory, the school's leader writes a few short notes explaining the situation and what actions the school's leadership team has taken to resolve problems and prevent errors in the future. Additionally, the column features short summaries of reports from the school's curriculum committee and data team about how closely the curriculum is aligned to the state standards (easy-to-collect quantitative data). Finally, the column concludes with a list of staff members and teams of teachers who play integral roles in keeping the school functioning at high reliability levels 1, 2, and 3.*

Resources for Level 3

A school might use the following resources (listed chronologically; most recent first) to facilitate work at level 3:

- *Vocabulary for the Common Core* (Marzano & Simms, 2013b)
- *Using Common Core Standards to Enhance Classroom Instruction and Assessment* (Marzano et al., 2013)
- *Teaching and Assessing 21st Century Skills* (Marzano & Heflebower, 2012)
- *Formative Assessment and Standards-Based Grading* (Marzano, 2010a)
- *Teaching Basic and Advanced Vocabulary: A Framework for Direct Instruction* (Marzano, 2010c)
- *Designing and Teaching Learning Goals and Objectives* (Marzano, 2009)

- *Designing and Assessing Educational Objectives: Applying the New Taxonomy* (Marzano & Kendall, 2008)

- *Making Standards Useful in the Classroom* (Marzano & Haystead, 2008)

- *The New Taxonomy of Educational Objectives* (Marzano & Kendall, 2007)

- *Classroom Assessment and Grading That Work* (Marzano, 2006)

- *Building Background Knowledge for Academic Achievement: Research on What Works in Schools* (Marzano, 2004)

- *What Works in Schools: Translating Research Into Action* (Marzano, 2003b)

- *Transforming Classroom Grading* (Marzano, 2000)

- *Content Knowledge: A Compendium of Standards and Benchmarks for K–12 Education* (Kendall & Marzano, 2000)

- *A Cluster Approach to Elementary Vocabulary Instruction* (Marzano & Marzano, 1988)

Other resources related to continually monitoring the viability of the curriculum, creating a comprehensive vocabulary program, and using direct instruction in knowledge application and metacognitive skills (the level 3 critical commitments); setting student achievement goals at the school level; analyzing and interpreting data to monitor school goals; and implementing intervention programs and practices can also be used.

Chapter 4

Standards-Referenced Reporting

• • •

Level 4 addresses how well a school's reporting system identifies specific subject and grade-level topics as well as each student's current status on those topics. A school that reaches level 4 high reliability status operates at a rarefied level because it reports student achievement in more detail than is possible with overall letter grades alone. Specifically, the school reports student achievement for specific topics (called *measurement topics*) within each subject area. Level 4 has two leading indicators:

4.1 Clear and measurable goals are established and are focused on critical needs regarding improving achievement of individual students within the school.

4.2 Data are analyzed, interpreted, and used to regularly monitor progress toward achievement goals for individual students.

A system in which student achievement is reported for specific measurement topics within each subject area is a *standards-referenced* reporting or grading system. Standards-referenced reporting systems, the focus of level 4, are frequently confused with *standards-based* or *competency-based* education systems, the focus of level 5. The difference between the two, and the reason that schools commonly work to achieve standards-referenced reporting (level 4) before moving toward a standards- or competency-based system (level 5), is that in a standards-referenced reporting system, students do not have to demonstrate proficiency in each measurement topic to move on to another level. In a standards- or competency-based education system, they do. Thus, standards-referenced reporting systems are an important step on the path to implementing a standards- or competency-based education system.

Level 4 Short-Form Leading Indicator Survey

Figure 4.1 (page 84) presents a short-form leading indicator survey for level 4. This survey can be administered to faculty, staff, and administrators within a school. The short-form survey provides very general information about a school's level 4 status. For more specific information, long-form surveys should be used.

1: Strongly disagree	2: Disagree	3: Neither disagree nor agree
4: Agree	5: Strongly agree	N: N/A or don't know

	1	2	3	4	5	N
4.1 Clear and measurable goals are established and are focused on critical needs regarding improving achievement of individual students within the school.	1	2	3	4	5	N
4.2 Data are analyzed, interpreted, and used to regularly monitor progress toward achievement goals for individual students.	1	2	3	4	5	N

Figure 4.1: Level 4 short-form leading indicator survey.

Level 4 Long-Form Leading Indicator Surveys

The level 4 long-form leading indicator surveys are designed to help gather specific data about a school's level 4 strengths and weaknesses. Reproducibles 4.1–4.4 (pages 85–88) contain the long-form surveys for level 4. Items should be added, deleted, or changed to meet the needs of individual schools.

Reproducible 4.1: Level 4 Long-Form Leading Indicator Survey for Teachers and Staff

1: Strongly disagree	2: Disagree	3: Neither disagree nor agree
4: Agree	5: Strongly agree	N: N/A or don't know

4.1 Clear and measurable goals are established and are focused on critical needs regarding improving achievement of individual students within the school.	Our school has articulated the essential elements for each subject area in the form of clear learning goals.	1	2	3	4	5	N
	Our school has created a proficiency scale for each essential element for each subject area.	1	2	3	4	5	N
	Our school has set goals for each student's achievement on state assessments, benchmark assessments, or common assessments.	1	2	3	4	5	N
	Our school has set goals for each student's knowledge gain on each proficiency scale.	1	2	3	4	5	N
	Each of my students knows his or her status on each of his or her achievement goals.	1	2	3	4	5	N
	Each of my students knows his or her status on each of his or her knowledge gain goals.	1	2	3	4	5	N
	Each of my students uses a data notebook to track his or her progress on individual goals.	1	2	3	4	5	N
	The parents of each of my students are aware of their child's individual goals.	1	2	3	4	5	N
	During student-led conferences, we focus on the student's individual goals.	1	2	3	4	5	N
	During parent-teacher conferences, we focus on the student's individual goals.	1	2	3	4	5	N
	My students perceive that their individual goals are academically challenging.	1	2	3	4	5	N
4.2 Data are analyzed, interpreted, and used to regularly monitor progress toward achievement goals for individual students.	I regularly analyze the status and growth of each of my students.	1	2	3	4	5	N
	Each of my students and his or her parents can describe the student's achievement status and growth status for each of the student's goals.	1	2	3	4	5	N
	I examine the individual achievement of my students from a value-added perspective.	1	2	3	4	5	N
	I report my students' results from multiple types of assessments to our school's leaders (for example, benchmark assessments or common assessments).	1	2	3	4	5	N
	I can describe the different types of individual student reports that are available to me.	1	2	3	4	5	N
	Someone in our school regularly updates student reports, graphs, and charts to track student achievement growth.	1	2	3	4	5	N
	My team regularly analyzes individual students' performance.	1	2	3	4	5	N

Reproducible 4.2: Level 4 Long-Form Leading Indicator Survey for Administrators

1: Strongly disagree	2: Disagree	3: Neither disagree nor agree
4: Agree	5: Strongly agree	N: N/A or don't know

4.1 Clear and measurable goals are established and are focused on critical needs regarding improving achievement of individual students within the school.	Our school has articulated the essential elements for each subject area in the form of clear learning goals.	1	2	3	4	5	N
	Our school has created a proficiency scale for each essential element for each subject area.	1	2	3	4	5	N
	Our school has set goals for each student's achievement on state assessments, benchmark assessments, or common assessments.	1	2	3	4	5	N
	Our school has set goals for each student's knowledge gain on each proficiency scale.	1	2	3	4	5	N
	Each student in our school knows his or her status on each of his or her achievement goals.	1	2	3	4	5	N
	Each student in our school knows his or her status on each of his or her knowledge gain goals.	1	2	3	4	5	N
	Each student in our school uses a data notebook to track his or her progress on individual goals.	1	2	3	4	5	N
	The parents of each student in our school are aware of their child's individual goals.	1	2	3	4	5	N
	During student-led conferences, students, teachers, and parents focus on the student's individual goals.	1	2	3	4	5	N
	During parent-teacher conferences, teachers and parents focus on the student's individual goals.	1	2	3	4	5	N
	All of the students in our school perceive that their individual goals are academically challenging.	1	2	3	4	5	N
4.2 Data are analyzed, interpreted, and used to regularly monitor progress toward achievement goals for individual students.	Each teacher in our school regularly analyzes the status and growth of each of his or her students.	1	2	3	4	5	N
	Each student in our school and his or her parents can describe the student's achievement status and growth status for each of the student's goals.	1	2	3	4	5	N
	I examine the individual achievement of students in our school from a value-added perspective.	1	2	3	4	5	N
	Each teacher in our school reports his or her students' results from multiple types of assessments to me (for example, benchmark assessments or common assessments).	1	2	3	4	5	N
	Each teacher in our school can describe the different types of individual student reports that are available to him or her.	1	2	3	4	5	N
	Someone in our school regularly updates student reports, graphs, and charts to track student achievement growth.	1	2	3	4	5	N
	Our school's leadership team regularly analyzes individual students' performance.	1	2	3	4	5	N

Reproducible 4.3: Level 4 Long-Form Leading Indicator Survey for Students

| 1: Strongly disagree | 2: Disagree | 3: Neither disagree nor agree |
| 4: Agree | 5: Strongly agree | N: N/A or don't know |

4.1 Clear and measurable goals are established and are focused on critical needs regarding improving achievement of individual students within the school.	There are clear learning goals I am expected to meet in each subject area.	1	2	3	4	5	N
	There is a proficiency scale for each goal I am expected to meet.	1	2	3	4	5	N
	I have goals for my performance on state assessments, benchmark assessments, or common assessments.	1	2	3	4	5	N
	I have goals for my knowledge gain on each proficiency scale.	1	2	3	4	5	N
	I know my current status on each of my achievement goals.	1	2	3	4	5	N
	I know my current status on each of my knowledge gain goals.	1	2	3	4	5	N
	I use a data notebook to track my progress on my goals.	1	2	3	4	5	N
	My parents know what my goals are.	1	2	3	4	5	N
	During student-led conferences, I talk about my goals.	1	2	3	4	5	N
	During parent-teacher conferences, my teacher and my parents talk about my goals.	1	2	3	4	5	N
	My goals are academically challenging.	1	2	3	4	5	N
4.2 Data are analyzed, interpreted, and used to regularly monitor progress toward achievement goals for individual students.	My teachers know my current status and growth on each of my goals.	1	2	3	4	5	N
	I can describe my achievement status and growth status for each of my goals.	1	2	3	4	5	N
	My teachers know how much I've grown as a result of their being my teachers.	1	2	3	4	5	N
	My teachers report my scores on exams, quizzes, and tests to my school's leaders.	1	2	3	4	5	N
	My teachers have reports that show how I am doing on my goals.	1	2	3	4	5	N
	When I make progress toward my goals, reports about me are updated.	1	2	3	4	5	N
	My teachers keep track of my progress toward my goals and help me move ahead if I'm not making progress.	1	2	3	4	5	N

Reproducible 4.4: Level 4 Long-Form Leading Indicator Survey for Parents

1: Strongly disagree	2: Disagree	3: Neither disagree nor agree
4: Agree	5: Strongly agree	N: N/A or don't know

4.1 Clear and measurable goals are established and are focused on critical needs regarding improving achievement of individual students within the school.	There are clear learning goals that my child is expected to meet in each subject area.	1	2	3	4	5	N
	There is a proficiency scale for each goal my child is expected to meet.	1	2	3	4	5	N
	My child has goals for his or her performance on state assessments, benchmark assessments, or common assessments.	1	2	3	4	5	N
	My child has goals for his or her knowledge gain on each proficiency scale.	1	2	3	4	5	N
	My child knows his or her current status on each of his or her achievement goals.	1	2	3	4	5	N
	My child knows his or her current status on each of his or her knowledge gain goals.	1	2	3	4	5	N
	My child uses a data notebook to track his or her progress on his or her goals.	1	2	3	4	5	N
	I know what my child's school goals are.	1	2	3	4	5	N
	During student-led conferences, my child talks about his or her school goals.	1	2	3	4	5	N
	During parent-teacher conferences, my child's teacher talks to me about my child's school goals.	1	2	3	4	5	N
	My child perceives his or her school goals as academically challenging.	1	2	3	4	5	N
4.2 Data are analyzed, interpreted, and used to regularly monitor progress toward achievement goals for individual students.	My child's teachers know my child's current status and growth on each of his or her goals.	1	2	3	4	5	N
	My child can describe his or her achievement status and growth status for each of his or her goals.	1	2	3	4	5	N
	My child's teachers know how much my child has grown as a result of their teaching.	1	2	3	4	5	N
	My child's teachers report my child's scores on exams, quizzes, and tests to the school's leaders.	1	2	3	4	5	N
	My child's teachers have reports that show how my child is doing on his or her goals.	1	2	3	4	5	N
	When my child makes progress toward his or her goals, reports about him or her are updated.	1	2	3	4	5	N
	My child's teachers keep track of my child's progress toward his or her goals and help my child move ahead if he or she is not making progress.	1	2	3	4	5	N

As with previous levels, teachers, staff, administrators, students, and parents complete the appropriate surveys in reproducibles 4.1–4.4 and school leaders examine the results to determine the leading indicators that should be the focus of initiatives and activities for level 4. For example, a school leader observes that survey responses indicate low levels of agreement with leading indicator 4.2, "Data are analyzed, interpreted, and used to regularly monitor progress toward achievement goals for individual students." Upon investigation, he finds that this is because teachers do not feel that the school's report card structure allows them to report students' growth in addition to their final status. In response, the leader works to redesign the report card so that it allows teachers to show students' status on each measurement topic at the beginning and end of each quarter. This is one of the critical commitments for level 4.

Level 4 Critical Commitments

Level 4 involves using report cards and other data reports that clearly communicate what students know and how much they have learned at school. To achieve high reliability status at level 4, we recommend two elements in this critical commitment: (1) develop proficiency scales for the essential content and (2) report status and growth on the report card using proficiency scales. Both represent major shifts in how schools are run.

Develop Proficiency Scales for the Essential Content

To execute a standards-referenced system of reporting, school leaders and teachers must think differently about how tests are designed and scored. Specifically, a school must design assessments that focus on a single topic or single dimension on which student achievement will be reported. As DuFour and Marzano (2011) noted,

> Whether teachers work independently or in groups, they typically design classroom assessments that cover multiple topics. For example, during a unit in an eighth-grade science class, a teacher might design an assessment that addresses two topics: (1) how climate patterns are affected by the water cycle and (2) how all the levels of the earth's atmosphere are affected by temperature and pressure. For the sake of discussion, let's assume that 35 percent of the points on the test address the first topic and 65 percent of the points address the second topic. Now let's consider two students, both of whom receive a score of 70 percent on the test. While their overall scores are the same, these two students might have a very different understanding of the content. (p. 121)

They go on to explain that one student—Student A—received a score of 70 by acquiring 35 of 35 points for the first topic and 35 of 65 points for the second topic. A second student—Student B—received the same score of 70 by acquiring 5 of 35 points for the first topic and 65 of 65 points for the second topic. DuFour and Marzano (2011) observed, "Clearly, the students have performed very differently on the two topics. Student A seems to know the first topic well, but not the second. Student B has the opposite profile" (p. 122). This practice creates a severe problem if one seeks to provide students with feedback on specific topics in each subject area. Proficiency scales are an effective way of overcoming the problem. (A detailed discussion of the effective use of proficiency scales can be found in Marzano, 2010a.)

The proficiency scale is a direct descendent of the rubric. Of course, the concept of a rubric has been around for many years. In the assessment world today, the term *rubric* usually applies to a description of knowledge or skills for a specific topic, such as the one shown in table 4.1 (page 90).

Table 4.1: Rubric for the Social Studies Topic of World War II at Grade 6

4	The student will create and defend a hypothesis about what might have happened if specific events that led to World War II had not happened or had happened differently.
3	The student will compare the primary causes for World War II with the primary causes for World War I.
2	The student will describe the primary causes for World War II.
1	The student will recognize isolated facts about World War II.

While rubrics like that in table 4.1 have been used successfully in individual classrooms, rubrics designed by different teachers are not usually comparable. To illustrate, consider table 4.2, which is a rubric written by a different teacher on the same topic and at the same grade level as the one in table 4.1.

Table 4.2: Second Rubric Regarding World War II at Grade 6

4	The student will compare the turning points in World War II to those in other wars.
3	The student will discuss key turning points in World War II that led to the victory of the Allied powers.
2	The student will recall basic information about how the Allied powers achieved a victory in World War II.
1	The student will recognize basic information about the outcome of World War II.

Even though the rubrics in tables 4.1 and 4.2 address the same topic (World War II), they have very different expectations regarding the content for scores 2, 3, and 4. In the first rubric, a score of 3 indicates that students can compare the causes of World War II with those of World War I. A score of 3 in the second rubric indicates that students can describe the turning points in World War II. That content is somewhat easier than the score 3 content in the first rubric.

To solve the problem of inconsistent rubrics from teacher to teacher, it is necessary to develop a systematic approach to rubric design. Such an approach is depicted in table 4.3.

Table 4.3: Generic Proficiency Scale

Score 4.0	More complex content
Score 3.0	Target learning goal
Score 2.0	Simpler content
Score 1.0	With help, partial success at score 2.0 content and score 3.0 content
Score 0.0	Even with help, no success

To understand the generic form of a proficiency scale shown in table 4.3, it is best to start with score 3.0. To receive a score of 3.0, a student must demonstrate competence regarding the target learning goal. A score of 2.0 indicates competence regarding simpler content, and a score of 4.0 indicates competence regarding more complex content. While scores 4.0, 3.0, and 2.0 involve different content, scores 1.0 and 0.0 do not. A score of 1.0 indicates that, independently, a student cannot demonstrate competence in the score 2.0 or 3.0 content, but, with help, he or she demonstrates partial competence. Score 0.0 indicates that even with help, a student does not demonstrate competence or skill in any of the content. The generic form of a proficiency scale allows for the creation of scales that are comparable across teachers, across topics, across subject areas, and across grade levels. See *Formative Assessment and Standards-Based Grading* (Marzano, 2010a) for more information on how proficiency scales designed using the generic framework in table 4.3 allow teachers to use three different types of classroom assessments (obtrusive, unobtrusive, and student-generated), compile summative scores for specific topics, and increase the reliability of test design and scoring.

Table 4.4 depicts a proficiency scale for the history topic of the role and emergence of the United States during World War II.

Table 4.4: Proficiency Scale for the Role and Emergence of the United States During World War II

Score 4.0	Students will explain and present specific examples of the continued evolution of the global role of the United States since World War II.
Score 3.0	Students will understand how the United States moved from isolationism to global superpower during, and as a result of, its role in World War II.
Score 2.0	Students will identify and explain concepts, people, and events related to the role of the United States in World War II and the post-war world (for example, *isolationism, neutrality, cash and carry, lend lease, Allies, D-Day, island hopping, total war, atomic bombs, Hiroshima, Nagasaki, Yalta Conference, Potsdam Conference, superpowers, United Nations, Marshall Plan, occupation of Japan*, and so on).
Score 1.0	With help, partial success at score 2.0 content and score 3.0 content
Score 0.0	Even with help, no success

Source: Adapted from Goshen Community School Corporation, 2011.

Regardless of who uses this scale, students' scores will be interpreted the same way in terms of their status relative to the learning goals articulated at score 3.0. A student who receives a score of 3.0 has met the learning goal, a student who receives a score of 4.0 has exceeded the learning goal, and so on.

Proficiency scales are foundational to reaching level 4 high reliability status, and their importance to successful school reform is evident in research literature. For example, in a study of minimum grading practices, Theodore Carey and James Carifio (2012) noted that if reforms are to "lead to fairer and more accurate and more consistent student assessment," they will need to involve "standards-based grading and proficiency scales, to address the inherent inequities now empirically established . . . to be a part of traditional grading schemes" (p. 207).

To achieve level 4 high reliability status, proficiency scales should be written for each essential topic in each course at each grade level. There are many resources to aid in such endeavors. For example, over 1,500 scales are available at **itembank.marzanoresearch.com** that address the subject areas of math, English language arts, science, U.S. history, world history, geography, economics, civics, world languages, visual arts, performing arts, physical education, technology, 21st century skills, social-emotional learning or life skills, and career and technical skills. Additionally, proficiency scales for the CCSS are available in the book *Using Common Core Standards to Enhance Classroom Instruction and Assessment* (Marzano et al., 2013).

Report Status and Growth on the Report Card Using Proficiency Scales

Ultimately, a school must address the issue of report cards if it is to reach high reliability status for level 4. A report card that would demonstrate such status is depicted in figure 4.2 (page 92).

Name:	John Mark	Grade Level:	4
Address:	123 Some Street	Homeroom:	Ms. Smith
City:	Anytown, CO 80000		

Language Arts (LA)	2.46	C	Participation	3.40	A	
Mathematics	2.50	B	Work Completion	2.90	B	
Science	2.20	C	Behavior	3.40	A	
Social Studies	3.10	A	Working in Groups	2.70	B	
Art	3.00	A				

		0.5	1.0	1.5	2.0	2.5	3.0	3.5	4.0
LA Reading									
Word Recognition and Vocabulary	2.5								
Reading for Main Idea	1.5								
Literary Analysis	2.0								
LA Writing									
Language Conventions	3.5								
Organization and Focus	2.5								
Research and Technology	1.0								
Evaluation and Revision	2.5								
Writing Applications	3.0								
LA Listening and Speaking									
Comprehension	3.0								
Organization and Delivery	3.0								
Analysis and Evaluation of Oral Media	2.5								
Speaking Applications	2.5								
Life Skills									
Participation	4.0								
Work Completion	3.5								
Behavior	3.5								
Working in Groups	3.0								
Average for Language Arts	2.46								

		0.5	1.0	1.5	2.0	2.5	3.0	3.5	4.0
Mathematics									
Number Systems	3.5								
Estimation	3.0								
Addition/Subtraction	2.5								
Multiplication/Division	2.5								
Ratio/Proportion/Percent	1.0								
Life Skills									
Participation	4.0								
Work Completion	2.0								
Behavior	3.5								
Working in Groups	2.0								
Average for Mathematics	2.50								

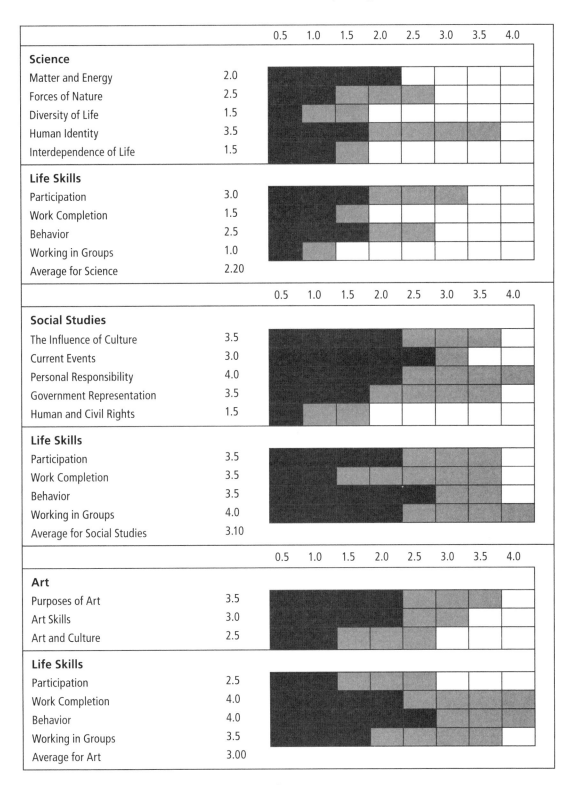

		0.5	1.0	1.5	2.0	2.5	3.0	3.5	4.0
Science									
Matter and Energy	2.0								
Forces of Nature	2.5								
Diversity of Life	1.5								
Human Identity	3.5								
Interdependence of Life	1.5								
Life Skills									
Participation	3.0								
Work Completion	1.5								
Behavior	2.5								
Working in Groups	1.0								
Average for Science	2.20								

		0.5	1.0	1.5	2.0	2.5	3.0	3.5	4.0
Social Studies									
The Influence of Culture	3.5								
Current Events	3.0								
Personal Responsibility	4.0								
Government Representation	3.5								
Human and Civil Rights	1.5								
Life Skills									
Participation	3.5								
Work Completion	3.5								
Behavior	3.5								
Working in Groups	4.0								
Average for Social Studies	3.10								

		0.5	1.0	1.5	2.0	2.5	3.0	3.5	4.0
Art									
Purposes of Art	3.5								
Art Skills	3.0								
Art and Culture	2.5								
Life Skills									
Participation	2.5								
Work Completion	4.0								
Behavior	4.0								
Working in Groups	3.5								
Average for Art	3.00								

Figure 4.2: Standards-referenced report card.

While this sample report card is for fourth grade, the same type of report card can easily be used from kindergarten up to grade 12. The primary difference at the high school level is that courses, as opposed to subject areas, are the focus of the report card.

Summative scores on topics are reported as bar graphs within each subject area. The student whose report card is shown in figure 4.2 (page 92) earned a summative score of 2.5 for *Word Recognition and Vocabulary* in language arts, a summative score of 3.0 for *Estimation* in mathematics, and so on. Note that the left side of each bar is darker than the right side. The darker portion represents a student's status at the beginning of the grading period, and the lighter portion represents the student's knowledge gain during the grading period.

Many schools employ traditional A, B, C, D, and F letter grades. To translate the average score on the proficiency scales addressed during a grading period for a specific subject into a letter grade, a simple guide is needed:

A = 3.00 to 4.00

B = 2.50 to 2.99

C = 2.00 to 2.49

D = 1.00 to 1.99

F = Below 1.00

It is important to remember when considering overall letter grades (commonly referred to as *omnibus grades*) that any attempt to summarize a student's status across a variety of topics involves decisions regarding where to end one grade designation and where to begin another. There is a logic to this system that is quite consistent with the design of the proficiency scale. Namely, the grade of A begins at 3.0 because a score of 3.0 indicates that a student has demonstrated understanding of all content in a target learning goal with no major errors or omissions. This makes some intuitive sense—if a student's average score indicates that he or she knows everything that was taught for the target learning goals, he or she should receive an A. The B grade range, 2.50 to 2.99, also has an intuitive logic to it. Having an average score within this range implies that across the learning goals addressed in a given grading period, the student typically demonstrated mastery of all of the basic content (score 2.0 content) and partial mastery of the score 3.0 content directly taught for the target learning goals.

Some schools like to use more refined categories such as A+, A, A−, and so on. If that is the case, the conversion scale depicted in table 4.5 can be used. A report card like the one in figure 4.2 (page 92) can be accompanied by a traditional transcript that lists courses taken, credits earned (in the case of high school), and an overall grade point average. As mentioned previously, this report card and variations of it are referred to as *standards-referenced* reporting. In a standards-referenced reporting system, students do not have to demonstrate proficiency in each measurement topic to move on to another grade level.

Proficiency scales and standards-referenced report cards both directly address the leading indicators for level 4. In effect, these two critical commitments make it rather easy to establish goals for individual students in the school (leading indicator 4.1) and monitor the progress of students toward those goals (leading indicator 4.2).

Level 4 Lagging Indicators

As at previous levels, lagging indicators and criterion scores must be formulated to track a school's progress toward and document its achievement of high reliability status for level 4, particularly for areas initially perceived as weak. The following are examples of statements that could be used as lagging indicators for level 4:

Table 4.5: Conversion Scale to Traditional Grades

Average Scale Score Across Multiple Goals	Traditional Grade
3.75–4.00	A+
3.26–3.74	A
3.00–3.25	A–
2.84–2.99	B+
2.67–2.83	B
2.50–2.66	B–
2.34–2.49	C+
2.17–2.33	C
2.00–2.16	C–
1.76–1.99	D+
1.26–1.75	D
1.00–1.25	D–
Below 1.00	F

- Written goals are available for each student in terms of his or her performance on state assessments, benchmark assessments, or common assessments.
- Documents articulating the learning progression (that is, proficiency scales) are available for each essential element of each subject area.
- Written goals are available for each student in terms of his or her knowledge gain regarding essential elements.
- Reports, charts, and graphs are available for each student depicting his or her status and growth on the chosen learning goals.
- Report cards display student status and growth on essential elements and individual learning goals.
- Eighty-five percent of students meet their growth goals each month.
- Eighty-five percent of parents report that they are aware of their child's growth goals.
- Eighty-five percent of parents report an understanding of the new report cards.
- Sixty percent of students grow an average of at least 1.5 score points in each subject area each grading period.

These are only examples of the type of lagging indicators a school might use. While there is no set number of lagging indicators a school should use, information gleaned from leading indicator surveys can help identify areas that are important to a school for which lagging indicators should be designed. Table 4.6 (page 96) will help facilitate the process of moving from leading to lagging indicators.

Table 4.6: Lagging Indicator Determination Chart for Level 4

Leading Indicators for Level 4	Used as Basis for a Lagging Indicator?	Lagging Indicator(s)	Criterion Score or Concrete Product
4.1 Clear and measurable goals are established and are focused on critical needs regarding improving achievement of individual students within the school.			
4.2 Data are analyzed, interpreted, and used to regularly monitor progress toward achievement goals for individual students.			

*Visit **marzanoresearch.com/reproducibles/leadership** to download a reproducible version of this form.*

School leaders select those leading indicators that are relevant to their school, create lagging indicators for each one, and set criterion scores for each lagging indicator. The examples that follow illustrate how various school leaders might complete this task in their schools.

Example 1

A middle school principal finds that faculty and staff responses to leading indicator 4.1, "Clear and measurable goals are established and are focused on critical needs regarding improving achievement of individual students within the school," are low. This isn't wholly surprising, since the only students for whom individual goals are established are those with IEPs. After talking to teachers and the school's guidance counselors, the principal creates a student advisory program to address the issue.

Each teacher in the school is assigned fifteen students. Initially, each student and teacher work together to start an academic goal sheet. Students' recent scores in math, language arts, science, and social studies are entered on the sheet, and the teacher and student work together to set goals that the student will work toward in the next month. Then, during a scheduled time once a month, each teacher meets with his or her advisory students to examine their progress toward their goals, talk about what they could do to achieve their goals faster or more easily, and set new goals if previous goals have been met. The principal collects copies of every student's sheet each month and reviews them to compile information about how many students are achieving their goals each month.

To measure progress, the principal designs a lagging indicator and criterion score: "Each month, 75 percent of students will achieve at least 75 percent of their goals in at least two content areas." The principal tracks students' progress monthly. To reach out to those students who consistently fail to achieve their goals, the principal meets with the student and his or her advisory teacher to figure out how the school can better support them.

Example 2

After finding that staff responses to leading indicator 4.2, "Data are analyzed, interpreted, and used to regularly monitor progress toward achievement goals for individual students," are low, a high school principal decides to implement a software program that will allow teachers to enter proficiency scales and track students' progress on them with the click of a button. The software also compiles reports for the principal at the end of each week to show which students have progressed on one or more proficiency scales.

To measure his school's progress, the principal creates a lagging indicator and criterion score: "Seventy percent of students will grow at least one level on at least one proficiency scale each week." Additionally, he creates a lagging indicator related to teachers' analyses of data: "All teachers will analyze and report three observations about their students' progress each week." Each teacher is required to examine his or her class's progress each week and send the principal three observations made from the data.

Example 3

After examining survey responses from teachers at her elementary school, a principal notices that scores are particularly low for leading indicator 4.1, "Clear and measurable goals are established and are focused on critical needs regarding improving achievement of individual students within the school." After taking a closer look at the survey items that received particularly low scores and talking to teachers, the principal recognizes that although the school has clearly articulated the learning goals for each grade level and subject area, a complete set of proficiency scales that clearly articulate the learning progression for each learning goal does not exist.

To remedy the situation, the principal begins by setting a lagging indicator to measure her school's success: "Proficiency scales articulating the learning progress for every learning goal at every grade level in every subject area are available." To work toward this goal, the principal first provides training to teachers on how to write clear, consistent proficiency scales. Then, she invites one teacher at each grade level and one teacher for special subjects (such as art, music, physical education, Spanish, and so on) to lead the proficiency scale creation process. These teachers are responsible for creating and asking their grade-level teammates to create proficiency scales for specific learning goals. Special subjects teachers agree to work with colleagues at other schools in the district to draft scales for their subject areas. Once the scales are drafted, the grade-level and subject-area teams review them and make any necessary changes. Then the team leader collects electronic copies of the scales in a designated folder on the school's network drive. This allows the principal to track teams' progress, provide her own feedback, and approve the final version of each scale. As various grade levels or subject areas finish scales for all of their learning goals, the principal compiles the scales into a single document and distributes electronic copies of the document to all teachers at that grade level or in that subject area.

Quick Data for Level 4

Achieving high reliability status for level 4 means that a school should collect quick data for that level as well as levels 3, 2, and 1. As with previous levels, quick data include quick conversations and quick observations as well as quantitative data. Quick data should be used for continuous monitoring of progress. We also provide suggestions for ways to acknowledge and celebrate success.

Quick Conversations

Quick conversations at level 4 could use the following questions:

4.1 Recently, to what extent have clear and measurable goals focused on critical needs regarding improving achievement of individual students within the school been established or updated?

4.2 Recently, to what extent have data been analyzed, interpreted, and used to regularly monitor progress toward achievement goals for individual students?

Collaborative team members might ask one or both of these questions to school community members over the course of a week (or another interval of time), code their responses, and record any notes from the conversation. The school's leadership team can then share information about the percentage of excellent, adequate, and unsatisfactory responses with the school community and celebrate successes on a regular basis.

Quick Observations

Additionally, quick observations could be made for level 4 indicators. Such observations should focus on recent incidents that indicate the following:

- Clear and measurable goals focused on critical needs regarding achievement of individual students within the school have been established.

- Clear and measurable goals focused on critical needs regarding achievement of individual students within the school have not been established.

- Data are analyzed, interpreted, and used to regularly monitor progress toward achievement goals for individual students.

- Data are not analyzed, interpreted, and used to regularly monitor progress toward achievement goals for individual students.

Collaborative team members gathering quick observations can use anecdotal notes to track the data they collect. The notes can be used to compose a short narrative summary of the incidents that were observed.

Easy-to-Collect Quantitative Data

In addition to quick conversations and quick observations, a school should take advantage of easy-to-collect level 4 quantitative data in order to continuously monitor level 4 performance. Such data might include the following:

- Quarterly reports of student performance on specific measurement topics
- Documents that continually track individual student progress toward essential learning goals
- Documents that continually track class progress toward essential learning goals
- Data-based decision-making protocol templates completed by teachers or teacher teams
- Mid-cycle progress reports of student achievement
- Student results on end-of-unit assessments that measure performance on specific measurement topics
- Weekly reports of student performance on specific measurement topics
- Regular reports of students' self-assessed performance on specific measurement topics

Acknowledging and Celebrating Success

Gathering data for levels 1, 2, 3, and 4 is the responsibility of schools who have achieved level 4 high reliability status. Additionally, school leaders should share quick data with the school community to acknowledge and celebrate the school's successes. The following vignette depicts how this might look in a level 4 school.

Mr. Proctor, the principal of a level 4 high reliability elementary school, has established specific times each month to share quick data with various members of his school's community. Every month, members of collaborative teams gather quick data on four indicators—one from each high reliability level the school has achieved. Then the principal shares quick data with staff members at the monthly staff meeting and with students. At the staff meeting, the collaborative team members who collected the quick data share the results and are invited to comment on their experiences while collecting it. During the meeting, Mr. Proctor also shares easy-to-collect quantitative data, such as notes from various students' goal-setting conferences. Periodically, Mr. Proctor shows students bar graphs with quick conversation data and tells a short story drawn from the school's quick observation data. He does this as part of his morning video announcement to all students. The principal always celebrates the accomplishments of at least one team of teachers, one class of students, one individual staff member, and one individual student in addition to at least one whole-school accomplishment. Students have learned to notice each row of the bar graphs and often come up to Mr. Proctor during the day and ask questions about how well the school is performing. To communicate quick data with parents and celebrate successes with the school community, Mr. Proctor uses his monthly update time at the school's PTO meeting to share the quick conversation bar graphs, easy-to-collect quantitative data, and quick observation narratives from the past four weeks with parents. He again highlights whole-school, team, class, staff member, and student accomplishments and encourages parents to ask questions or give additional feedback about any quick data topic.

Resources for Level 4

A school might use the following resources (listed chronologically; most recent first) to facilitate work at level 4:

- *A School Leader's Guide to Standards-Based Grading* (Heflebower, Hoegh, & Warrick, 2014)
- *Using Common Core Standards to Enhance Classroom Instruction and Assessment* (Marzano et al., 2013)
- *Leaders of Learning: How District, School, and Classroom Leaders Improve Student Achievement* (DuFour & Marzano, 2011)
- *Formative Assessment and Standards-Based Grading* (Marzano, 2010a)
- *Designing and Teaching Learning Goals and Objectives* (Marzano, 2009)
- *Designing and Assessing Educational Objectives: Applying the New Taxonomy* (Marzano & Kendall, 2008)
- *Making Standards Useful in the Classroom* (Marzano & Haystead, 2008)
- *Classroom Assessment and Grading That Work* (Marzano, 2006)
- *Designing a New Taxonomy of Educational Objectives* (Marzano, 2001)
- *Transforming Classroom Grading* (Marzano, 2000)
- *A Comprehensive Guide to Designing Standards-Based Districts, Schools, and Classrooms* (Marzano & Kendall, 1996)

Other resources related to developing proficiency scales for essential content and reporting status and growth on the report card using proficiency scales (the critical commitments for level 4), analyzing and interpreting data to monitor individual students' goals, and other level 4 topics can also be used.

Chapter 5
Competency-Based Education

● ● ●

Level 5 addresses the extent to which a school matriculates students based on their demonstrated competence rather than on the amount of time they have spent learning. In other words, students only move to the next level when they have demonstrated competence at the previous level. Level 5 status represents the most rarefied level of high reliability designation; once a school has achieved this level, it will have implemented competency-based education (also called standards-based education). Level 5 has three leading indicators:

5.1 Students move on to the next level of the curriculum for any subject area only after they have demonstrated competence at the previous level.

5.2 The school schedule is designed to accommodate students moving at a pace appropriate to their situation and needs.

5.3 Students who have demonstrated competency levels greater than those articulated in the system are afforded immediate opportunities to begin work on advanced content and/or career paths of interest.

The most straightforward approach to implementing a competency-based system while maintaining traditional grade levels is to treat grade levels as performance levels. Each grade level represents a level of knowledge or skill defined by specific learning goals for which proficiency scales have been developed. It is important to note that, within this approach, a student will be operating at different grade levels for different subject areas.

Level 5 Short-Form Leading Indicator Survey

Figure 5.1 (page 102) presents a short-form leading indicator survey for level 5. This survey can be administered to faculty, staff, and administrators within a school. The short-form survey provides very general information about a school's level 5 status. For more specific information, long-form surveys should be used.

| 1: Strongly disagree | 2: Disagree | 3: Neither disagree nor agree |
| 4: Agree | 5: Strongly agree | N: N/A or don't know |

5.1 Students move on to the next level of the curriculum for any subject area only after they have demonstrated competence at the previous level.	1	2	3	4	5	N
5.2 The school schedule is designed to accommodate students moving at a pace appropriate to their situation and needs.	1	2	3	4	5	N
5.3 Students who have demonstrated competency levels greater than those articulated in the system are afforded immediate opportunities to begin work on advanced content and/or career paths of interest.	1	2	3	4	5	N

Figure 5.1: Level 5 short-form leading indicator survey.

Level 5 Long-Form Leading Indicator Surveys

The level 5 long-form leading indicator surveys are designed to gather specific data about a school's level 5 strengths and weaknesses. Reproducibles 5.1–5.4 (pages 103–106) contain the long-form surveys for level 5. Survey items can be added, deleted, or changed to meet the individual needs of schools.

Reproducible 5.1: Level 5 Long-Form Leading Indicator Survey for Teachers and Staff

1: Strongly disagree	2: Disagree	3: Neither disagree nor agree
4: Agree	5: Strongly agree	N: N/A or don't know

5.1 Students move on to the next level of the curriculum for any subject area only after they have demonstrated competence at the previous level.	Our school has established minimum scores (criterion scores) that students must meet to demonstrate competence for each essential element of the curriculum.	1	2	3	4	5	N
	Our school has a system in place to track each student's status on each essential element in each subject area.	1	2	3	4	5	N
	I continually monitor each of my students' status for each essential element in the subject areas I teach.	1	2	3	4	5	N
	When a student reaches the criterion score for all essential elements at a particular level in a subject area, he or she immediately starts working on elements at the next level.	1	2	3	4	5	N
5.2 The school schedule is designed to accommodate students moving at a pace appropriate to their situation and needs.	Our school has replaced grade levels with competency levels or allows students to work at different grade levels for different subject areas.	1	2	3	4	5	N
	Our school has multiple venues simultaneously available where students can learn the essential elements for each level of each subject area.	1	2	3	4	5	N
	Our school has multiple venues simultaneously available where students can demonstrate competency with the essential elements for each level of each subject area.	1	2	3	4	5	N
	Online competency-based instruction and assessment are available at our school for each essential element at each level in each subject area.	1	2	3	4	5	N
	Someone at our school constantly monitors how long it takes each student to move through the levels of each subject area.	1	2	3	4	5	N
5.3 Students who have demonstrated competency levels greater than those articulated in the system are afforded immediate opportunities to begin work on advanced content and/or career paths of interest.	Any student who has demonstrated the highest level of competence for a subject area has opportunities for advanced study in that subject area.	1	2	3	4	5	N
	Any student who has demonstrated competence adequate for high school graduation can begin working on and receive credit for college-level work.	1	2	3	4	5	N
	Any student who has demonstrated competence adequate for high school graduation can begin working on and receive credit for work toward a trade or career area of interest to him or her.	1	2	3	4	5	N

Reproducible 5.2: Level 5 Long-Form Leading Indicator Survey for Administrators

1: Strongly disagree	2: Disagree	3: Neither disagree nor agree
4: Agree	5: Strongly agree	N: N/A or don't know

5.1 Students move on to the next level of the curriculum for any subject area only after they have demonstrated competence at the previous level.	Our school has established minimum scores (criterion scores) that students must meet to demonstrate competence for each essential element of the curriculum.	1	2	3	4	5	N
	Our school has a system in place to track each student's status on each essential element in each subject area.	1	2	3	4	5	N
	Each teacher in our school continually monitors each of his or her students' statuses for each essential element in the subject areas he or she teaches.	1	2	3	4	5	N
	When a student reaches the criterion score for all essential elements at a particular level in a subject area, he or she immediately starts working on elements at the next level.	1	2	3	4	5	N
5.2 The school schedule is designed to accommodate students moving at a pace appropriate to their situation and needs.	Our school has replaced grade levels with competency levels or allows students to work at different grade levels for different subject areas.	1	2	3	4	5	N
	Our school has multiple venues simultaneously available where students can learn the essential elements for each level of each subject area.	1	2	3	4	5	N
	Our school has multiple venues simultaneously available where students can demonstrate competency with the essential elements for each level of each subject area.	1	2	3	4	5	N
	Online competency-based instruction and assessment are available at our school for each essential element at each level in each subject area.	1	2	3	4	5	N
	Someone at our school constantly monitors how long it takes each student to move through the levels of each subject area.	1	2	3	4	5	N
5.3 Students who have demonstrated competency levels greater than those articulated in the system are afforded immediate opportunities to begin work on advanced content and/or career paths of interest.	Any student who has demonstrated the highest level of competence for a subject area has opportunities for advanced study in that subject area.	1	2	3	4	5	N
	Any student who has demonstrated competence adequate for high school graduation can begin working on and receive credit for college-level work.	1	2	3	4	5	N
	Any student who has demonstrated competence adequate for high school graduation can begin working on and receive credit for work toward a trade or career area of interest to him or her.	1	2	3	4	5	N

Reproducible 5.3: Level 5 Long-Form Leading Indicator Survey for Students

| 1: Strongly disagree | 2: Disagree | 3: Neither disagree nor agree |
| 4: Agree | 5: Strongly agree | N: N/A or don't know |

5.1 Students move on to the next level of the curriculum for any subject area only after they have demonstrated competence at the previous level.	I know what I must do to show that I have mastered each learning goal or essential element.	1	2	3	4	5	N
	My school keeps track of how well I am doing on each learning goal or essential element.	1	2	3	4	5	N
	My teachers keep track of how well I am doing on each learning goal or essential element I am studying in their classes.	1	2	3	4	5	N
	When I have mastered every learning goal or essential element at one level, I move on to the next level.	1	2	3	4	5	N
5.2 The school schedule is designed to accommodate students moving at a pace appropriate to their situation and needs.	I can work at different competency levels or grade levels for different subject areas.	1	2	3	4	5	N
	There are several different ways for me to work on a specific learning goal or essential element.	1	2	3	4	5	N
	I can demonstrate that I have mastered a specific learning goal or essential element in several different ways.	1	2	3	4	5	N
	One of the ways I can work on learning goals is by taking classes and tests on the computer.	1	2	3	4	5	N
	Someone at my school keeps track of how long it takes me to master all the learning goals or essential elements in each level of each subject area.	1	2	3	4	5	N
5.3 Students who have demonstrated competency levels greater than those articulated in the system are afforded immediate opportunities to begin work on advanced content and/or career paths of interest.	Once I have mastered all the learning goals for all the levels of a subject area, I can work on advanced studies in that subject area.	1	2	3	4	5	N
	Once I have mastered all the learning goals that I need to graduate, I can begin working on and receive credit for college-level work.	1	2	3	4	5	N
	Once I have mastered all the learning goals that I need to graduate, I can work on a career or trade area that is interesting to me and earn credit for my work.	1	2	3	4	5	N

Reproducible 5.4: Level 5 Long-Form Leading Indicator Survey for Parents

| 1: Strongly disagree | 2: Disagree | 3: Neither disagree nor agree |
| 4: Agree | 5: Strongly agree | N: N/A or don't know |

		1	2	3	4	5	N
5.1 Students move on to the next level of the curriculum for any subject area only after they have demonstrated competence at the previous level.	My child's school has set minimum scores for each essential element (or learning goal) that my child must meet to demonstrate competence with it.	1	2	3	4	5	N
	My child's school has a system to track my child's status on each essential element (or learning goal) in each subject area.	1	2	3	4	5	N
	My child's teachers continually monitor his or her status for each essential element (or learning goal) in the subject areas they teach.	1	2	3	4	5	N
	When my child reaches the criterion score for all the essential elements (or learning goals) at a particular level in a subject area, he or she immediately starts working on elements at the next level.	1	2	3	4	5	N
5.2 The school schedule is designed to accommodate students moving at a pace appropriate to their situation and needs.	My child's school has replaced grade levels with competency levels or allows students to work at different grade levels for different subject areas.	1	2	3	4	5	N
	My child has opportunities to learn the essential elements for each level of each subject area in several different ways that are always available.	1	2	3	4	5	N
	My child has opportunities to demonstrate competency with the essential elements for each level of each subject area in several different ways that are always available.	1	2	3	4	5	N
	Online classes and tests are available at my child's school for each essential element at each level in each subject area.	1	2	3	4	5	N
	Someone at my child's school constantly monitors how long it takes my child to move through the levels of each subject area.	1	2	3	4	5	N
5.3 Students who have demonstrated competency levels greater than those articulated in the system are afforded immediate opportunities to begin work on advanced content and/or career paths of interest.	If my child demonstrates the highest level of competence for a subject area, he or she can work on advanced studies in that area.	1	2	3	4	5	N
	If my child demonstrates competence adequate for high school graduation, he or she can begin working on and receive credit for college-level work.	1	2	3	4	5	N
	If my child demonstrates competence adequate for high school graduation, he or she can begin working on and receive credit for work toward a trade or career area that interests him or her.	1	2	3	4	5	N

Using survey results, school leaders can determine the leading indicators that should be the focus of activities and initiatives for level 5. For example, when a school leader found that survey results were low for leading indicator 5.2, "The school schedule is designed to accommodate students moving at a pace appropriate to their situation and needs," he decided to implement flex scheduling, which facilitates students' work at different levels for different subjects. A student could be at competency level 6 (or grade 6) for mathematics, but at competency level 8 (or grade 8) for English language arts. A flexible schedule that allows students to move through content at their own pace is part of a critical commitment for level 5: getting rid of time requirements to move through levels of knowledge.

Level 5 Critical Commitments

To achieve high reliability status at level 5, school leaders will need to eliminate time requirements for moving through levels of knowledge. There are two elements to this critical commitment: (1) get rid of time requirements and (2) adjust reporting systems accordingly.

Get Rid of Time Requirements

The driving force behind a competency-based system is that students do not move on to the next level until they have demonstrated competence at the previous level. Additionally, each student progresses at his or her individual pace. This revolutionary concept has been advocated and discussed by many with a number of variations on the theme (for example, Bloom, 1976; Boyer, 1983, 1995; Goodlad, 1984; Guskey, 1980, 1985, 1987; Spady, 1988, 1994, 1995) but is most commonly associated with the work of John Carroll (1963, 1989). The Carroll model can be represented using the following formula:

$$\text{Amount of learning} \ = \ \frac{\text{Time actually spent}}{\text{Time needed to learn}}$$

This formula indicates that the amount of content any student learns about a given topic is a function of the time the student actually spends focusing on the content and the time needed to learn the content. If a student has spent five hours on a topic but needs ten hours to learn the content, then she has not learned the content well.

An interesting issue disclosed by Carroll's formula is the fact that students require differing amounts of time to learn content. This is innately problematic. It seems almost self-evident that an optimal educational system would be one in which students could take as much or as little time as needed to learn important content.

As described in the book *Classroom Assessment and Grading That Work* (Marzano, 2006), there are at least two conventions in the current system that work against the realization of Carroll's model—grade levels and credits. By definition, grade levels work against students progressing through content at their own pace. Regardless of their understanding of and skill with the content addressed at a given grade level, all students, with some rare exceptions, are moved through the system at exactly the same pace. Time in school is constant; learning is varied.

Using credits as the basic indicator of progress within a subject area at the secondary level also works against the realization of a competency-based system. Students must spend a specific amount of time in a course to receive credit for the course. Credits can be traced back over one hundred years to 1906, when Henry S. Pritchett, the president of the Carnegie Foundation for the Advancement of Teaching, "defined a 'unit' as 'a course of five periods weekly throughout an academic year'" (as cited in Tyack & Tobin, 1994, p. 460). In his book, *High School: A Report on Secondary Education in America*, Ernest Boyer (1983) explained that the credit approach has spawned a virtual "logjam" (p. 237) in terms of allowing students to progress through subject areas at their own pace.

Adjust Reporting Systems Accordingly

As described in *Formative Assessment and Standards-Based Grading* (Marzano, 2010a), a competency-based system does not lock students into a specific grade level based on their age. Rather, students move up and down a continuum of knowledge or skills based on their demonstrated competence for each subject area. Table 5.1 depicts an individual student's report card in this version of a competency-based system. This report card indicates the student's status across various subject areas.

In *Formative Assessment and Standards-Based Grading*, Marzano (2010a) described the type of report card shown in table 5.1:

> Most subject areas include levels 1 to 10. Level 10 represents mastery of the content expected for a general high school diploma. Not all subject areas have ten levels, however. Art has six levels, technology has seven levels, and personal/social skills has five levels. This convention is used because in a standards-based system, content is not organized into grade levels that are based on age. It is instead organized into levels based on the nature of the content. While the content necessary for high school graduation might logically fall into ten levels for some subjects, it might fall into fewer levels for others. (pp. 119–120)

Another feature of this report card is the manner in which a student's current status is reported. In mathematics, for example, the student's score at level 4 is reported as a ratio of "21 of 35." This means that the student has achieved a score of 3.0 or higher on twenty-one of the thirty-five learning goals (that is, proficiency scales) at that level. This student must demonstrate score 3.0 or higher competence on fourteen more proficiency scales to progress to level 5 in mathematics. Finally, each subject area can also include advanced levels. Art has one advanced level, career literacy has two advanced levels, math and language arts each have three advanced levels, and so on.

No overall grades are computed in competency-based systems because they are antithetical to the competency-based philosophy. In a competency-based system, the emphasis is on demonstrating proficiency in each and every learning goal before a student progresses to the next level. Overall grades simply summarize a student's average competence across a set of topics across a given level and subject area.

For some schools and districts, getting rid of traditional grade levels represents too radical a shift from the norm. Stated differently, some schools seek to employ a competency-based approach but maintain traditional grade levels. Fortunately, there is a straightforward way to do this: treat grade levels as performance levels. The record-keeping system up to grade 8 in such a system is depicted in table 5.2 (page 110).

Table 5.1: Competency-Based Report Card

Level	Art	Career Literacy	Mathematics	Personal/Social Skills	Language Arts	Science	Social Studies	Technology
Advanced 3	n/a	n/a		n/a			n/a	n/a
Advanced 2	n/a			n/a				
Advanced 1								
10	n/a			n/a				n/a
09	n/a			n/a				n/a
08	n/a			n/a				n/a
07	n/a			n/a				
06				n/a				
05								
04		2 of 16	21 of 35		3 of 36	17 of 25		
03	9 of 10	3.0 (Proficient)	3.0 (Proficient)	4 of 6	4.0 (Advanced)	3.0 (Proficient)	13 of 15	7 of 8
02	3.0 (Proficient)	3.0 (Proficient)	4.0 (Advanced)	3.0 (Proficient)	3.0 (Proficient)	3.0 (Proficient)	3.0 (Proficient)	4.0 (Advanced)
01	3.0 (Proficient)	3.0 (Proficient)	4.0 (Advanced)	3.0 (Proficient)	3.0 (Proficient)	3.0 (Proficient)	3.0 (Proficient)	3.0 (Proficient)

Source: Marzano, 2010a, p. 119.

Table 5.2: Competency-Based Reporting for Grades K–8

Level	Art	Career Literacy	Mathematics	Personal/ Social Skills	Language Arts	Science	Social Studies	Technology
Grade 8								
Grade 7								
Grade 6								
Grade 5			4 of 32					
Grade 4		7 of 11	3.0 (Proficient)		7 of 31	2 of 23		
Grade 3		3.0 (Proficient)	4.0 (Advanced)	2 of 6	3.0 (Proficient)	4.0 (Advanced)		
Grade 2	9 of 10	3.0 (Proficient)	3.0 (Proficient)	3.0 (Proficient)	4.0 (Advanced)	3.0 (Proficient)	2 of 15	7 of 8
Grade 1	3.0 (Proficient)	3.0 (Proficient)	4.0 (Advanced)	3.0 (Proficient)	3.0 (Proficient)	3.0 (Proficient)	3.0 (Proficient)	4.0 (Advanced)
Grade K	3.0 (Proficient)	3.0 (Proficient)	4.0 (Advanced)	3.0 (Proficient)	3.0 (Proficient)	3.0 (Proficient)	3.0 (Proficient)	3.0 (Proficient)

Source: Adapted from Marzano, 2010a, p. 121.

Table 5.2 is basically identical to table 5.1 (page 109) except that it uses grade levels. Each grade level represents a level of knowledge or skill defined by specific learning goals for which proficiency scales have been developed.

Table 5.3 depicts a competency-based report card at the high school level.

Table 5.3: Competency-Based Reporting for High School

Subject Area	Course	Score
Mathematics	Calculus	
	Geometry	
	Algebra II	12 of 24
	Algebra I	3.0 (Proficient)
Science	AP Environmental Science	
	Physics	
	Chemistry	6 of 22
	Biology	3.0 (Proficient)
Social Studies	Economics	
	World History	11 of 21
	U.S. History	4.0 (Advanced)
	Geography	3.0 (Proficient)
Language Arts	Shakespeare	
	Ancient Literature	13 of 22
	European Literature	3.0 (Proficient)
	U.S. Literature	3.0 (Proficient)
Art	Orchestra	
	Performing Arts	9 of 21
	Painting	3.0 (Proficient)
Technology	Digital Graphics and Animation	
	Desktop Publishing	17 of 22
	Computer Science	4.0 (Advanced)

Source: Marzano, 2010a, p. 121.

At the high school level, specific courses are listed for each subject area in the order of their complexity. For example, in mathematics, Algebra I addresses simpler content than Algebra II, and so on. At the high school level, some courses may not exhibit a strict hierarchic structure. For example, in technology, Desktop

Publishing may not have to be taken before Digital Graphics and Animation. Therefore, some courses at the high school level will not have prerequisite courses or be prerequisites to other courses. However, progression through any course is still executed in a competency-based fashion. Once a student has demonstrated mastery (score 3.0 content) for all of the proficiency scales within a course, the student receives credit for that course. As is the case with a competency-based system that does not use grade levels, overall omnibus grades are not assigned to students when grade levels are used as performance levels. Rather, the report cards depicted in tables 5.1 (page 109) and 5.3 (page 111) are kept current at all times, and a ratio is recorded at each grade level in which the student is working for each subject area.

Examining the patterns in tables 5.1, 5.2, and 5.3, it is evident that the lowest acceptable score a student can receive on any proficiency scale for any level, grade level, or course is a 3.0. This is because students must demonstrate a score of 3.0 on all topics to move on to the next level, grade level, or course. However, discriminations can still be made between students as to their performances within each level, grade level, or course. To illustrate, consider table 5.2 (page 110). Notice that at grade 1, the student achieved an overall score of "advanced" in mathematics and technology and an overall score of "proficient" in all other subjects. Recall that at each grade level, students are scored on a four-point scale for each learning goal. If a student has achieved a 4.0 on all (or the majority) of the learning goals for a given subject at a given grade level, he or she can be awarded the status of "advanced" as opposed to "proficient."

The critical commitments for level 5, getting rid of time requirements and adjusting reporting systems accordingly, make it possible for students to move to the next level only after demonstrating competence at the previous level (leading indicator 5.1), facilitate a school schedule that accommodates students moving at an appropriate pace (leading indicator 5.2), and allow students who have demonstrated competency levels beyond those articulated in the system to work on advanced content and career paths (leading indicator 5.3).

Level 5 Lagging Indicators

The following are examples of lagging indicators for level 5.

- A written master plan is available articulating the essential elements at each level for each subject area.
- Reports are available that indicate each student's current status for each essential element at each level for each subject area.
- A written master plan is available articulating the alternate pathways a student might take to learn and demonstrate competence in each essential element at each level for each subject area.
- A written master plan is available articulating how students can pursue advanced content, work on college credit, and pursue careers of interest once they have demonstrated competence at all levels of the system.
- Reports are available depicting how long each student is taking to move through the curriculum for each subject area at each level.
- Reports are available depicting how long, on average, students are taking to move through the curriculum for each subject area at each level.
- Fifteen percent of students matriculate through the system at least one year earlier than they would have in a traditional system.
- Ninety-five percent of students take the same amount of time or less to matriculate through the system than they would have in a traditional system.

Again, these are only examples of the type of lagging indicators a school might use. Table 5.4 can facilitate the process of moving from leading indicators to lagging indicators.

Table 5.4: Lagging Indicator Determination Chart for Level 5

Leading Indicators for Level 5	Used as Basis for a Lagging Indicator?	Lagging Indicator(s)	Criterion Score or Concrete Product
5.1 Students move on to the next level of the curriculum for any subject area only after they have demonstrated competence at the previous level.			
5.2 The school schedule is designed to accommodate students moving at a pace appropriate to their situation and needs.			
5.3 Students who have demonstrated competency levels greater than those articulated in the system are afforded immediate opportunities to begin work on advanced content and/or career paths of interest.			

*Visit **marzanoresearch.com/reproducibles/leadership** to download a reproducible version of this form.*

School leaders should select leading indicators relevant to their school, create lagging indicators for each one, and set criterion scores for each lagging indicator. The following examples depict how school leaders might do this.

Example 1

After administering surveys for level 5, a middle school principal notices that the average score for leading indicator 5.2, "The school schedule is designed to accommodate students moving at a pace appropriate to their situation and needs," is only 1.8. The principal and the other school leaders interview various members of the school community and realize that although the schedule is designed to accommodate students moving at their own pace through competency levels, a number of students are stalled out at specific levels. In some cases, students have been working on one level of one subject area for more than a year. The school leadership team realizes that it needs to implement a system that tracks how long it takes each student to move through each level of the curriculum so that teachers can provide interventions if students are moving too slowly.

To measure the success of their efforts, the principal and leadership team design a lagging indicator and criterion score: "Ninety-five percent of students take the same amount of time or less to matriculate through the system than they would have in a traditional system." The leadership team creates a process to collect data about how quickly students are progressing through the system. It divides the number of learning goals at each level by the number of instructional days available in each year. This allows teachers to calculate how quickly each student needs to progress through each level in order to take the same amount of time or less to graduate as they would have taken in a traditional system. For students who are behind and need to catch up, the school's leaders work with special education teachers and other instructional support staff to design targeted interventions that will help students fill gaps and progress to where they need to be to graduate on time or earlier.

The school leadership team also selects three of its members to compile data about how quickly each student is progressing through the system every two weeks. After the first data collection, 5 percent of students are on track to matriculate in less time than would be required by a traditional system, 80 percent of students are on track to matriculate in the same amount of time as a traditional system, and 15 percent of students will require more time than a traditional system. The school continues to implement interventions with the 15 percent of students who are behind schedule and within three months, only 10 percent of students are behind schedule. By the end of the school year, the school has met its lagging indicator. The data collection team is left in place so that if students fall behind schedule in the future, they can quickly be identified and interventions can be implemented.

Example 2

An elementary school principal notices that scores for leading indicator 5.1, "Students move on to the next level of the curriculum for any subject area only after they have demonstrated competence at the previous level," are particularly low on surveys from parents. After interviewing several parents and teachers, she realizes that the school's reporting system isn't clearly communicating students' current status or their level of competence (proficient or advanced) for previous levels. Although the school adjusted its report cards when it achieved level 4 high reliability status, changes need to be made now that it is working on level 5.

To work toward leading indicator 5.1, the principal and teacher leaders design a concrete lagging indicator: "Report cards will clearly state how many learning goals (out of how many are required) a student has achieved for the level he or she is working on in each subject area and will clearly state whether he or she was proficient or advanced on previous levels." The principal works with the school's electronic gradebook provider and district directors to redesign the school's report card to include the information stated in the lagging indicator. She also holds focus groups with parents before the new report card is used to determine how easy it is to interpret and how much information parents can glean about what a student is doing well with, what he or she still needs to work on, and where he or she needs extra help. She also interviews teachers to find out how easy it is to enter students' scores and progress and if they feel the new report card gives them opportunities to communicate necessary information to parents.

Because the school's lagging indicator for report cards is concrete, the principal is able to examine the report card and see that it clearly meets the parameters stated in the lagging indicator. However, she wants to make sure that the report card adequately meets students', teachers', and parents' needs; therefore, she designs a quick data question to be used whenever report cards are sent to parents: "To what extent does the report card give you a clear picture of what level a student is working on, where he or she is in that level, and how well he or she has done on previous levels?" She codes each response as *excellent, adequate,* or *unsatisfactory.* After the first use of the new report cards, the principal and leadership team only get a few unsatisfactory responses; most are adequate or excellent. To ensure that the report card continues to meet the lagging indicator, the principal implements a system to collect feedback each time report cards are sent to parents. If feedback indicates that they are not well understood or do not provide useful information, she and the teacher leaders make adjustments accordingly.

Example 3

A high school principal whose school is working on level 5 high reliability status reviews survey data and sees that the average score for leading indicator 5.3, "Students who have demonstrated competency levels greater than those articulated in the system are afforded immediate opportunities to begin work on advanced content and/or career paths of interest," is lower than 3.0. He asks students, parents, and teachers for feedback and finds that students who have completed all of the competency levels for some subjects (such as music, drama, dance, foreign languages, and computer programming) do not have opportunities for advanced studies in those areas. Instead, they are encouraged to focus on moving more rapidly through core subjects such as English, mathematics, science, and social studies, since those areas do have opportunities for advanced studies. Students with special interests in non-core subjects are left without outlets for further study once they complete the requirements for graduation.

To address this area of need, the principal first designs a lagging indicator to measure the school's success: "All content areas will have at least two levels of advanced study available for students who meet the requirements for graduation." To work toward this indicator, the principal asks the head of each department without advanced levels to meet with him to discuss next steps. For music, the choir director recommends that the school purchase electronic composition software and hardware along with tutorials that will allow advanced students to study college-level musical theory and composition. For drama, the theater director recommends that advanced students complete a set of learning goals that will require them to write, direct, and produce a short play or drama. In computer programming, the school's technology director suggests enrolling students in massive open online courses (MOOCs) taught by professors at Stanford, Harvard, MIT, and other universities. One by one, the principal works with teacher leaders in each department to design levels of advanced study for students who have completed graduation requirements for that area.

By the end of three months, each subject area has at least one level of advanced study and a distinct set of learning goals with proficiency scales to measure students' progress. In many cases, students can earn college or technical study credit for their work. By the end of five months, each subject area has at least two levels of advanced study, and in at least one of those levels, students can earn college or technical study credit.

Quick Data for Level 5

A school that has achieved level 5 high reliability status is functioning at a high level. To ensure that the school continues to function at the highest levels of effectiveness and reliability, the school's leaders will need to collect quick data for all five high reliability levels. Although the amount of data they need to collect is significantly greater than that of schools at lower levels, the same strategies, quick conversations, quick observations, and easy-to-collect quantitative data can still be used for continuous monitoring. We also provide suggestions for ways to acknowledge and celebrate success.

Quick Conversations

Quick conversations at level 5 could feature the following questions:

5.1 Recently, to what extent has it been apparent that students move on to the next level of the curriculum for any subject area only after they have demonstrated competence at the previous level?

5.2 Recently, to what extent has it been apparent that the school schedule is designed to accommodate students moving at a pace appropriate to their situation and needs?

    5.3 Recently, to what extent has it been apparent that students who have demonstrated competency levels greater than those articulated in the system are afforded immediate opportunities to begin work on advanced content and/or career paths of interest?

Collaborative team members ask one or more of these questions to the school community (along with questions from the other four levels) during a given interval of time. Coded responses and notes are compiled by the leadership team and shared with the school's community to celebrate successes.

Quick Observations

Quick observations for level 5 should include recent incidents that indicate the following:

- Students move on to the next level of the curriculum for any subject area only after they have demonstrated competence at the previous level.

- Students do not move on to the next level of the curriculum for any subject area after they have demonstrated competence at the previous level.

- The school schedule is designed to accommodate students moving at a pace appropriate to their situation and needs.

- The school schedule is not designed to accommodate students moving at a pace appropriate to their situation and needs.

- Students who have demonstrated competency levels greater than those articulated in the system are afforded immediate opportunities to begin work on advanced content and career paths of interest.

- Students who have demonstrated competency levels greater than those articulated in the system are not afforded immediate opportunities to begin work on advanced content and career paths of interest.

Quick observations can be collected using anecdotal notes. Notes can then be summarized in a short narrative.

Easy-to-Collect Quantitative Data

In addition to quick conversations and quick observations, a school should take advantage of easy-to-collect level 5 quantitative data that can be used to continuously monitor level 5 performance. Such data might include the following:

- Quarterly reports of the number of students progressing to the next level for specific subject areas

- Reports on the success of students meeting individualized education plans

- Schedules depicting access to teachers (for example, ninety minutes once a week for remediation or extensions)

- Course guides noting options for students (AP, International Baccalaureate, honors courses)

- Reports of the number of students working on college-level coursework

- Reports on the number of college credits students earned each term

- Records for the number of students working on career prep opportunities

- Quarterly reports of students attaining mastery of specific achievement goals within a subject area

- Regular technology-enhanced reports on student progress toward increased levels of attainment for specific subject areas

- Regular technology-enhanced reports on expected student progress toward increased levels of attainment for specific subject areas
- Reports on the number of students taking advanced online coursework offered by institutes of higher learning

Acknowledging and Celebrating Success

As stated previously, schools who have achieved level 5 high reliability status should collect quick data for all five high reliability levels. Quick data should be regularly shared with the school community and successes celebrated. The following vignette depicts how this might look in a level 5 high school.

> At Silver Mountain High School, one collaborative team collects quick conversation data from its fellow teachers on a monthly basis and a different collaborative team is responsible for collecting quick observation data. However, Dr. Park, the principal, feels that not enough quick data are being collected from students and parents. To remedy this issue, he establishes a monthly poll on the school's website. Each month, five featured quick conversation questions (one for each level of high reliability status) are posted on the school's website and an email is sent to all students and parents asking them to respond to the questions. Respondents rate each question as excellent, adequate, or unsatisfactory and can write notes to explain their answers. At the end of each month, a staff member compiles the responses and posts them on the website, along with easy-to-collect quantitative data (such as how many students moved to the next level of a content area that month) and the next month's questions.
>
> Each month, Dr. Park compiles all quick data into a narrative summary, posts them on the school's website as a PDF, and distributes it to all teachers as printed copies. Teachers are encouraged to post the quick data results in their classrooms and to celebrate successes with students. Based on quick data, Dr. Park arranges for specific celebrations. At the monthly all-staff meeting, he recognizes the accomplishments of the whole school and individual teachers and staff members. At school assemblies, Dr. Park celebrates the accomplishments of the whole school, individual teachers and staff members, and individual students. At his bimonthly business luncheon with community members and leaders, he shares quick data results and celebrates the successes of the whole school and certain community members and parents (who are specifically invited to attend the luncheon). In the front hallway of the school, school leaders display a running record of the quick data collected for the year and various celebrations that have taken place.

Resources for Level 5

A school might use the following resources (listed chronologically; most recent first) to facilitate work at level 5:

- *Using Common Core Standards to Enhance Classroom Instruction and Assessment* (Marzano et al., 2013)
- *Formative Assessment and Standards-Based Grading* (Marzano, 2010a)
- *Delivering on the Promise: The Education Revolution* (DeLorenzo, Battino, Schreiber, & Carrio, 2009)
- *Making Standards Useful in the Classroom* (Marzano & Haystead, 2008)
- *Classroom Assessment and Grading That Work* (Marzano, 2006)

- *Transforming Classroom Grading* (Marzano, 2000)
- *A Comprehensive Guide to Designing Standards-Based Districts, Schools, and Classrooms* (Marzano & Kendall, 1996)

Other resources related to getting rid of time requirements and adjusting reporting systems accordingly (the critical commitments for level 5), accommodating an appropriate pace for students, creating opportunities for students to work on advanced content or careers, and other level 5 topics can also be used.

Epilogue

Achieving high reliability status is no small feat, and schools will need to invest time, resources, and ingenuity to reach their goals. However, becoming a high reliability school is worth the effort. Consider level 2 status. At level 2, a school guarantees that all teachers are using effective instructional techniques. Having effective teachers in each classroom not only improves student achievement (Nye, Konstantopoulos, & Hedges, 2004) but can also influence the future earning potential of students, as noted by Michael Strong (2011):

> A teacher who is significantly above average in effectiveness can generate annual marginal gains of over $400,000 in present value of student earnings. Expressed another way, replacing the bottom 5% to 8% of teachers with teachers of average effectiveness could move the United States to near the top of the international math and science rankings. (p. 8)

Each level has specific tangible benefits that will improve a school's effectiveness and therefore the lives of its students. How then should school leaders who want to achieve all five levels of high reliability status proceed? Here, we present five guidelines that will facilitate fairly rapid movement through the levels.

Guideline 1: Provide a General Overview of the High Reliability Process to Teachers, Staff, and Administrators

The high reliability process described in this handbook is not the typical way schools in the United States have approached reform or quality control. Consequently, teachers, staff members, and administrators in a school should be provided with an overview of the process and engage in a dialogue about the process.

The introduction of this book provides a viable overview. A principal might download that chapter at **marzanoresearch.com/hrs** and ask all teachers, staff members, and administrators in the school to read it prior to having an open discussion. During an open discussion about the advisability of embarking on the high reliability process, teachers, staff members, and administrators might be asked questions like the following:

- How would the high reliability process positively affect our school?
- What would we have to change about ourselves to embark on the high reliability process?
- What are we currently doing as a school that relates to the high reliability process?
- What will we give up or put on hold to engage in the high reliability process?
- Why is the high reliability process worth considering at our school?

Once answers to questions like these have been discussed, it is useful to ask teachers, staff members, and administrators about their level of commitment to such a process. In general, the level of commitment should be relatively strong to successfully complete the process.

Guideline 2: Select Leading and Lagging Indicators That Are Appropriate for Your School

The leading and lagging indicators described in previous chapters are examples only. Certainly, a school leader should not attempt to address all of them. Such an effort would be counterproductive. Rather, school leaders should select, adapt, or create only those leading and lagging indicators that will most positively influence their students and fit best with the culture and needs of their school. In many cases, leading and lagging indicators will be implicit in the school's mission, vision, and goals.

Guideline 3: Work on Levels 1, 2, and 3 Simultaneously, but Seek High Reliability Status for One Level at a Time

Levels 1, 2, and 3 are obviously related because they are a natural part of the day-to-day running of a school. Safety and order are always concerns in a well-run school, and cooperation and collaboration (or lack thereof) always influence day-to-day operations (level 1). Instruction occurs every day, and the more attention paid to enhancing instructional practices in the classroom, the better (level 2). The curriculum is what teachers and students interact about on a daily basis, and the more attention paid to ensuring that the curriculum is guaranteed and viable and focused on enhancing student learning, the better (level 3). In short, school leaders are, by definition, engaged in level 1, 2, and 3 activities constantly, and anything they can do to improve their school's status regarding these levels is always a step in the right direction. Consequently, a school leader could work on level 1, level 2, or level 3 leading indicators simultaneously. For example, to increase a school's effectiveness, a school leader decides to install an electronic tool to help collect suggestions and comments from teachers as to the effective running of the school—a level 1 leading indicator. In addition, the school leader decides to develop a document that describes a schoolwide model of instruction—a level 2 leading indicator. Finally, the school leader also decides to determine which elements of the CCSS are considered essential learning goals for each grade level—a level 3 leading indicator. Improvement in various aspects of levels 1, 2, and 3 using the leading indicators as guides is always good practice as long as these efforts do not overload teachers and school leaders.

Establishing criteria and collecting evidence for high reliability status for a particular level, however, should be done methodically and systematically, level by level, starting at level 1. For example, using level 1 survey results, a school leader identifies the lagging indicators the school will use for level 1 and the criterion scores for those indicators. Interventions are identified and implemented as needed. Next, the school leader collects evidence indicating that the school has met the criterion scores for each selected lagging indicator. Once the criterion scores for all selected lagging indicators are met, the school leader considers the school validated for level 1 high reliability status and moves on to level 2.

One final point to make about moving through the levels is that many schools are already operating highly effectively regarding levels 1 through 3. Consequently, attaining high reliability status for these levels might simply be a matter of collecting evidence for selected lagging indicators. In effect, schools that suspect they are already operating at high reliability status for a given level should be able to identify lagging indicators and criterion scores and confirm their perceptions in a quick and efficient manner.

Guideline 4: If Necessary, Set Interim Criterion Scores for Lagging Indicators

Some school leaders find it useful to set criterion scores for lagging indicators in a staged or incremental fashion to provide a scaffold for reaching their ultimate goal. To illustrate, consider the following lagging indicator for level 1: "Few, if any, incidents occur in which rules and procedures are not followed." A school leader might ultimately wish to establish as the criterion for high reliability status that the school must average no more than one incident of a significant violation of school rules and procedures per month. However, after examining the school's records, the school leader realizes that the school is currently far from reaching that status. To provide momentum for progress on this lagging indicator, the school leader sets a goal of moving to an average of no more than five violations per month as an interim step.

Guideline 5: Lead From the Perspective of the Indicators

Throughout this book, we have consistently alluded to the role of school leaders in moving a school through the five levels. Ultimately, whether a school reaches high reliability status for any level is dependent on whether the school leaders keep the five high reliability levels at the forefront of their efforts to guide the school in its improvement efforts. In effect, school leaders should judge their effectiveness by the extent to which they systematically move their school toward meeting criterion scores for the lagging indicators. Such a perspective will keep the school and its leaders firmly grounded in tangible results that have direct effects on the well-being of students.

The following vignette depicts a school that has attained high reliability status on all five levels.

> *Las Palmas High School recently attained high reliability status for level 5. Over the past several years, it identified and addressed areas of weakness regarding safety and collaboration in the school (level 1), effective teaching in every classroom (level 2), guaranteed and viable curriculum (level 3), standards-referenced reporting (level 4), and, finally, competency-based education (level 5). Students now matriculate based on their demonstrated mastery of specific learning goals for each level of each subject area. Report cards clearly report students' current status and growth on learning goals at their current level. Teachers who teach the same subject use the same learning goals and assessments to assign grades, and the curriculum is carefully monitored to ensure that it is possible to teach all the content in the instructional time available. The school's leaders observe and coach teachers toward improvement on specific goals from the schoolwide model of effective instruction, and teachers work together in collaborative teams to address issues of school safety and gather input about the school's functioning from all members of the school's community.*
>
> *Now that the school has achieved all five levels, school leaders collect quick data to monitor their performance, prevent problems, and resolve errors quickly if they arise. Each month, one collaborative team in the school is assigned to collect quick data for each level. Since the school has ten collaborative teams, five teams (one per level) collect quick data one month, and five collect them the next month. When it is a team's turn to collect data, it is assigned a level. The team can select specific members to collect data, or all members can collect data. Each team is expected to collect quick conversation data from eight to ten members of the school community on at least two questions related to its assigned level. The principal meets with teams to help them design quick conversation questions. Teams are also expected to collect quick observation data for incidents related to their levels. At the end of the month, teams report their data to an assistant principal, who compiles them into a report along with*

easily accessible quantitative data such as counts of rule infractions, average scores on teacher evaluation protocols, reports from the school's curriculum committee, reports of student performance on specific measurement topics, and reports of the number of students who have progressed to the next level in certain subject areas. This report is shared with the faculty at staff meetings where successes are celebrated. The principal uses the report to tell stories and recognize the accomplishments of individuals, teams, and the school as a whole.

The report is also used to address areas of weakness. For example, one month the report showed a rise in discipline infractions, an area of quick data related to level 1. The principal investigated the issue and discovered that the building had hosted a higher number of substitute teachers that month than normal, and that many of the month's discipline infractions were from classes with substitute teachers. To address the problem, the school's leadership team designed a set of guidelines to help teachers prepare appropriate lesson plans for substitutes and another set of guidelines to help substitute teachers better handle discipline issues.

In conclusion, K–12 schools in the United States have traditionally not operated from a high reliability perspective, even though such a perspective is characteristic of virtually every organization that provides consistent, high-quality, high-yield results. Yet there is nothing stopping schools from doing so. Using this handbook, leaders can guide their schools to unprecedented levels of performance.

References and Resources

Ambady, N., & Rosenthal, R. (1992). Thin slices of expressive behavior as predictors of interpersonal consequences: A meta-analysis. *Psychological Bulletin, 111*(2), 256–274.

Beck, I. L., & McKeown, M. G. (1985). Teaching vocabulary: Making the instruction fit the goal. *Educational Perspectives, 23*(1), 11–15.

Bellamy, G. T., Crawford, L., Marshall, L. H., & Coulter, G. A. (2005). The fail-safe schools challenge: Leadership possibilities from high reliability organizations. *Educational Administration Quarterly, 41*(3), 383–412.

Bloom, B. S. (1976). *Human characteristics and school learning.* New York: McGraw-Hill.

Bosker, R. J. (1992). *The stability and consistency of school effects in primary education.* Enschede, Overijssel, The Netherlands: University of Twente.

Bosker, R. J., & Witziers, B. (1995, January). *School effects, problems, solutions and a meta-analysis.* Paper presented at the International Congress for School Effectiveness and Improvement, Leeuwarden, Friesland, The Netherlands.

Bosker, R. J., & Witziers, B. (1996, April). *The magnitude of school effects, Or: Does it really matter which school a student attends?* Paper presented at the annual meeting of the American Educational Research Association, New York.

Boyer, E. L. (1983). *High school: A report on secondary education in America.* New York: Harper & Row.

Boyer, E. L. (1995). *The basic school: A community for learning.* Princeton, NJ: Carnegie Foundation for the Advancement of Teaching.

Brookover, W. B., Beady, C., Flood, P., Schweitzer, J., & Wisenbaker, J. (1979). *School social systems and student achievement: Schools can make a difference.* New York: Praeger.

Brookover, W. B., Schweitzer, J. H., Schneider, J. M., Beady, C. H., Flood, P. K., & Wisenbaker, J. M. (1978). Elementary school social climate and school achievement. *American Educational Research Journal, 15*(2), 301–318.

Bryk, A. S., & Raudenbush, S. W. (1992). *Hierarchical linear models: Applications and data analysis methods.* Newbury Park, CA: SAGE.

Bryk, A. S., Sebring, P. B., Allensworth, E., Luppescu, S., & Easton, J. Q. (2010). *Organizing schools for improvement: Lessons from Chicago.* Chicago: University of Chicago Press.

Burstein, L. (Ed.). (1992). *The IEA study of mathematics III: Student growth and classroom processes.* New York: Pergamon Press.

Carey, T., & Carifio, J. (2012). The minimum grading controversy: Results of a quantitative study of seven years of grading data from an urban high school. *Educational Researcher, 41*(6), 201–208.

Carroll, J. B. (1963). A model of school learning. *Teachers College Record, 64*(8), 723–733.

Carroll, J. B. (1989). The Carroll model: A 25-year retrospective and prospective view. *Educational Researcher, 18*(1), 26–31.

Coleman, J. S., Campbell, E. Q., Hobson, C. J., McPartland, J., Mood, A. M., Weinfield, F. D., et al. (1966). *Equality of educational opportunity.* Washington, DC: U.S. Department of Health, Education, and Welfare, Office of Education.

Costa, A. L., & Kallick, B. (Eds.). (2009). *Habits of mind across the curriculum: Practical and creative strategies for teachers.* Alexandria, VA: Association for Supervision and Curriculum Development.

Creemers, B. P. M. (1994). *The effective classroom.* London: Cassell.

DeLorenzo, R. A., Battino, W. J., Schreiber, R. M., & Carrio, B. G. (2009). *Delivering on the promise: The education revolution.* Bloomington, IN: Solution Tree Press.

DuFour, R., & Marzano, R. J. (2011). *Leaders of learning: How district, school, and classroom leaders improve student achievement.* Bloomington, IN: Solution Tree Press.

Eberts, R. W., & Stone, J. A. (1988). Student achievement in public schools: Do principals make a difference? *Economics of Education Review, 7*(3), 291–299.

Edmonds, R. (1979a). *A discussion of the literature and issues related to effective schooling.* Cambridge, MA: Center for Urban Studies, Harvard Graduate School of Education.

Edmonds, R. (1979b). Effective schools for the urban poor. *Educational Leadership, 37*(1), 15–27.

Edmonds, R. (1979c). Some schools work and more can. *Social Policy, 9,* 28–32.

Edmonds, R. (1981a). Making public schools effective. *Social Policy, 12,* 56–60.

Edmonds, R. (1981b). *A report on the research project, "Search for effective schools . . ." and certain of the designs for school improvement that are associated with the project.* Unpublished report prepared for NIE. East Lansing: Institute for Research on Teaching, College of Education, Michigan State University.

Foley, E., Mishook, J., Thompson, J., Kubiak, M., Supovitz, J., & Rhude-Faust, M. K. (n.d.). *Beyond test scores: Leading indicators for education.* Providence, RI: Annenberg Institute for School Reform, Brown University.

Gallup. (2013). *Gallup student poll questions.* Accessed at www.gallupstudentpoll.com/156431/gallup-student-poll-questions.aspx on November 5, 2013.

Goldstein, H. (1997). Methods of school effectiveness research. *School Effectiveness and School Improvement, 8*(4), 369–395.

Good, T. L., & Brophy, J. E. (1986). School effects. In M. C. Wittrock (Ed.), *Handbook of research on teaching* (3rd ed., pp. 570–602). New York: Macmillan.

Goodlad, J. L. (1984). *A place called school: Prospects for the future.* New York: McGraw-Hill.

Goshen Community School Corporation. (2011). *WWII (Emergence of U.S.).* Accessed at www.marzanoresearch.com/media/document/file/ss-us-history-hs-8.pdf on February 26, 2014.

Guskey, T. R. (1980). What is mastery learning? *Instructor, 90*(3), 80–86.

Guskey, T. R. (1985). *Implementing mastery learning.* Belmont, CA: Wadsworth.

Guskey, T. R. (1987). Rethinking mastery learning reconsidered. *Review of Educational Research, 57*(2), 225–229.

Hattie, J. A. C. (2009). *Visible learning: A synthesis of over 800 meta-analyses relating to achievement.* New York: Routledge.

Hattie, J. A. C. (2012). *Visible learning for teachers: Maximizing impact on learning.* New York: Routledge.

Heflebower, T., Hoegh, J. K., & Warrick, P. (with Hoback, M., McInteer, M., & Clemens, B.). (2014). *A school leader's guide to standards-based grading.* Bloomington, IN: Marzano Research.

Husén, T. (Ed.). (1967a). *International study of achievement in mathematics, a comparison of twelve countries: Volume 1.* New York: Wiley.

Husén, T. (Ed.). (1967b). *International study of achievement in mathematics, a comparison of twelve countries: Volume 2.* New York: Wiley.

Jencks, C., Smith, M., Acland, H., Bane, M. J., Cohen, D., Gintis, H., et al. (1972). *Inequality: A reassessment of the effect of family and schooling in America.* New York: Basic Books.

Kendall, J. S., & Marzano, R. J. (2000). *Content knowledge: A compendium of standards and benchmarks for K–12 education* (3rd ed.). Alexandria, VA: Association for Supervision and Curriculum Development.

Levine, D. U., & Lezotte, L. W. (1990). *Unusually effective schools: A review and analysis of research and practice.* Madison, WI: National Center for Effective Schools Research and Development.

Linde, J. A., Jeffery, R. W., French, S. A., Pronk, N. P., & Boyle, R. G. (2005). Self-weighing in weight gain prevention and weight loss trials. *Annals of Behavioral Medicine, 30*(3), 210–216.

Locke, E. A., & Latham, G. P. (2002). Building a practically useful theory of goal setting and task motivation: A 35-year odyssey. *American Psychologist, 57*(9), 705–717.

Luyten, H. (1994). *School effects: Stability and malleability.* Enschede, Overijssel, The Netherlands: University of Twente.

Madaus, G. F., Kellaghan, T., Rakow, E. A., & King, D. J. (1979). The sensitivity of measures of school effectiveness. *Harvard Educational Review, 49*(2), 207–230.

Magaña, S., & Marzano, R. J. (2014). *Enhancing the art & science of teaching with technology.* Bloomington, IN: Marzano Research.

Marzano, R. J. (1992). *A different kind of classroom: Teaching with dimensions of learning.* Alexandria, VA: Association for Supervision and Curriculum Development.

Marzano, R. J. (2000). *Transforming classroom grading.* Alexandria, VA: Association for Supervision and Curriculum Development.

Marzano, R. J. (2001). *Designing a new taxonomy of educational objectives.* Thousand Oaks, CA: Corwin Press.

Marzano, R. J. (with Marzano, J. S., & Pickering, D. J.). (2003a). *Classroom management that works: Research-based strategies for every teacher.* Alexandria, VA: Association for Supervision and Curriculum Development.

Marzano, R. J. (2003b). *What works in schools: Translating research into action.* Alexandria, VA: Association for Supervision and Curriculum Development.

Marzano, R. J. (2004). *Building background knowledge for academic achievement: Research on what works in schools.* Alexandria, VA: Association for Supervision and Curriculum Development.

Marzano, R. J. (2006). *Classroom assessment and grading that work.* Alexandria, VA: Association for Supervision and Curriculum Development.

Marzano, R. J. (2007). *The art and science of teaching: A comprehensive framework for effective instruction.* Alexandria, VA: Association for Supervision and Curriculum Development.

Marzano, R. J. (2009). *Designing and teaching learning goals and objectives*. Bloomington, IN: Marzano Research.

Marzano, R. J. (2010a). *Formative assessment and standards-based grading*. Bloomington, IN: Marzano Research.

Marzano, R. J. (Ed.). (2010b). *On excellence in teaching*. Bloomington, IN: Solution Tree Press.

Marzano, R. J. (2010c). *Teaching basic and advanced vocabulary: A framework for direct instruction*. Boston: Cengage ELT.

Marzano, R. J. (with Boogren, T., Heflebower, T., Kanold-McIntyre, J., & Pickering, D.). (2012a). *Becoming a reflective teacher*. Bloomington, IN: Marzano Research.

Marzano, R. J. (2012b). The two purposes of teacher evaluation. *Educational Leadership, 70*(3), 14–19.

Marzano, R. J., Brandt, R., Hughes, C., Jones, B., Presseisen, B., Rankin, S., et al. (1988). *Dimensions of thinking: A framework for curriculum and instruction*. Alexandria, VA: Association for Supervision and Curriculum Development.

Marzano, R. J., Frontier, T., & Livingston, D. (2011). *Effective supervision: Supporting the art and science of teaching*. Alexandria, VA: Association for Supervision and Curriculum Development.

Marzano, R. J., & Haystead, M. W. (2008). *Making standards useful in the classroom*. Alexandria, VA: Association for Supervision and Curriculum Development.

Marzano, R. J., & Heflebower, T. (2012). *Teaching and assessing 21st century skills*. Bloomington, IN: Marzano Research.

Marzano, R. J., & Kendall, J. S. (1996). *A comprehensive guide to designing standards-based districts, schools, and classrooms*. Alexandria, VA: Association for Supervision and Curriculum Development.

Marzano, R. J., & Kendall, J. S. (2007). *The new taxonomy of educational objectives* (2nd ed.). Thousand Oaks, CA: Corwin Press.

Marzano, R. J., & Kendall, J. S. (2008). *Designing and assessing educational objectives: Applying the new taxonomy*. Thousand Oaks, CA: Corwin Press.

Marzano, R. J., & Marzano, J. (1988). *A cluster approach to elementary vocabulary instruction*. Newark, DE: International Reading Association.

Marzano, R. J., & Pickering, D. J. (1997). *Dimensions of learning: Teacher's manual* (2nd ed.). Alexandria, VA: Association for Supervision and Curriculum Development.

Marzano, R. J., & Pickering, D. J. (with Heflebower, T.). (2011). *The highly engaged classroom*. Bloomington, IN: Marzano Research.

Marzano, R. J., Pickering, D. J., & Pollock, J. E. (2001). *Classroom instruction that works: Research-based strategies for increasing student achievement*. Alexandria, VA: Association for Supervision and Curriculum Development.

Marzano, R. J., & Pollock, J. E. (2001). Standards-based thinking and reasoning skills. In A. L. Costa (Ed.), *Developing minds: A resource book for teaching thinking* (3rd ed., pp. 29–34). Alexandria, VA: Association for Supervision and Curriculum Development.

Marzano, R. J., & Simms, J. A. (2013a). *Coaching classroom instruction*. Bloomington, IN: Marzano Research.

Marzano, R. J., & Simms, J. A. (2013b). *Vocabulary for the Common Core*. Bloomington, IN: Marzano Research.

Marzano, R. J., & Simms, J. A. (2014). *Questioning sequences in the classroom*. Bloomington, IN: Marzano Research.

Marzano, R. J., & Toth, M. (2013). *Teacher evaluation that makes a difference: A new model for teacher growth and student achievement*. Alexandria, VA: Association for Supervision and Curriculum Development.

Marzano, R. J., & Waters, T. (2009). *District leadership that works: Striking the right balance*. Bloomington, IN: Solution Tree Press.

Marzano, R. J., Waters, T., & McNulty, B. A. (2005). *School leadership that works: From research to results*. Alexandria, VA: Association for Supervision and Curriculum Development.

Marzano, R. J., Yanoski, D. C., Hoegh, J. K., & Simms, J. A. (with Heflebower, T., & Warrick, P.). (2013). *Using Common Core standards to enhance classroom instruction and assessment*. Bloomington, IN: Marzano Research.

Mortimore, P., Sammons, P., Stoll, L., Lewis, D., & Ecob, R. (1988). *School matters: The junior years*. Chicago: Open Books.

National Commission on Excellence in Education. (1983). *A nation at risk: The imperative for educational reform: A report to the nation and the Secretary of Education, United States Department of Education*. Washington, DC: U.S. Government Printing Office.

Nye, B., Konstantopoulos, S., & Hedges, L. V. (2004). How large are teacher effects? *Educational Evaluation and Policy Analyses, 26*(3), 237–257.

Partnership for 21st Century Skills. (2012). *Framework for 21st century learning*. Accessed at www.p21.org/our -work/p21-framework on January 23, 2013.

Pellegrino, J. W., & Hilton, M. L. (Eds.). (2012). *Education for life and work: Developing transferable knowledge and skills in the 21st century*. Washington, DC: National Academies Press.

Purkey, S. C., & Smith, M. S. (1983). Effective schools: A review. *The Elementary School Journal, 83*(4), 426–452.

Raudenbush, S. W., & Bryk, A. S. (1988). Methodological advances in analyzing the effects of schools and classrooms on student learning. In E. Z. Rothkopf (Ed.), *Review of research in education: Vol. 15* (pp. 423–475). Washington, DC: American Educational Research Association.

Raudenbush, S. W., & Willms, J. D. (1995). The estimation of school effects. *Journal of Educational and Behavioral Statistics, 20*(4), 307–335.

Reynolds, D., & Teddlie, C. (2000a). Linking school effectiveness and school improvement. In C. Teddlie & D. Reynolds (Eds.), *The international handbook of school effectiveness research* (pp. 206–231). New York: Falmer Press.

Reynolds, D., & Teddlie, C. (2000b). The process of school effectiveness. In C. Teddlie & D. Reynolds (Eds.), *The international handbook of school effectiveness research* (pp. 134–159). New York: Falmer Press.

Rickover, H. G. (1959). *Education and freedom*. New York: Dutton.

Rowe, K. J., & Hill, P. W. (1994, March). *Multilevel modeling in school effectiveness research: How many levels?* Paper presented at the Seventh International Congress for School Effectiveness and Improvement, Melbourne, Victoria, Australia.

Rowe, K. J., Hill, P. W., & Holmes-Smith, P. (1995). Methodological issues in educational performance and school effectiveness research: A discussion with worked examples. *Australian Journal of Education, 39*(3), 217–248.

Rutter, M., Maughan, B., Mortimore, P., Ouston, J., & Smith, A. (1979). *Fifteen thousand hours: Secondary schools and their effects on children*. Cambridge, MA: Harvard University Press.

Sammons, P. (1999). *School effectiveness: Coming of age in the twenty-first century.* Lisse, South Holland, The Netherlands: Swets and Zeitlinger.

Sammons, P., Hillman, J., & Mortimore, P. (1995). *Key characteristics of effective schools: A review of school effectiveness research.* London: Office of Standards in Education and Institute of Education.

Scheerens, J. (1992). *Effective schooling: Research, theory and practice.* London: Cassell.

Scheerens, J., & Bosker, R. J. (1997). *The foundations of educational effectiveness.* New York: Pergamon Press.

Spady, W. G. (1988). Organizing for results: The basis of authentic restructuring and reform. *Educational Leadership, 46*(2), 4–8.

Spady, W. G. (1994). Choosing outcomes of significance. *Educational Leadership, 51*(6), 18–22.

Spady, W. G. (1995). Outcome-based education: From instructional reform to paradigm restructuring. In H. H. Block, S. T. Everson, & T. Guskey (Eds.), *School improvement programs* (pp. 367–398). New York: Scholastic.

Stringfield, S. (1995). Attempts to enhance students' learning: A search for valid programs and high-reliability implementation techniques. *School Effectiveness and School Improvement, 6*(1), 67–96.

Stringfield, S., Reynolds, D., & Schaffer, E. C. (2008). *Improving secondary students' academic achievement through a focus on reform reliability: Four- and nine-year findings from the High Reliability Schools project.* Berkshire, England: CfBT Education Trust. Accessed at http://cdn.cfbt.com/~/media/cfbtcorporate/files/research/2008/r-improving-secondary-students-academic-achievement-2008.pdf on October 28, 2013.

Stringfield, S., Reynolds, D., & Schaffer, E. (2012). Making best practice standard—and lasting. *Phi Delta Kappan, 94*(1), 45–50.

Stringfield, S., & Teddlie, C. (1989). The first three phases of the Louisiana school effectiveness study. In B. P. M. Creemers, T. Peters, & D. Reynolds (Eds.), *School effectiveness and school improvement: Proceedings of the Second International Congress, Rotterdam* (pp. 281–294). Lisse, South Holland, The Netherlands: Swets and Zeitlinger.

Strong, M. (2011). *The highly qualified teacher: What is teacher quality and how do we measure it?* New York: Teachers College Press.

Tomlinson, C. A., & Imbeau, M. B. (2010). *Leading and managing a differentiated classroom.* Alexandria, VA: Association for Supervision and Curriculum Development.

Townsend, T. (Ed.). (2007a). *International handbook of school effectiveness and improvement: Part one.* Dordrecht, South Holland, The Netherlands: Springer.

Townsend, T. (Ed.). (2007b). *International handbook of school effectiveness and improvement: Part two.* Dordrecht, South Holland, The Netherlands: Springer.

Tyack, D. K., & Tobin, W. (1994). The "grammar" of schooling: Why has it been so hard to change? *American Educational Research Journal, 31*(3), 453–479.

U.S. Department of Labor, Secretary's Commission on Achieving Necessary Skills. (1991). *What work requires of schools: A SCANS report for America 2000.* Washington, DC: Author. Accessed at http://wdr.doleta.gov/SCANS/whatwork/whatwork.pdf on January 23, 2013.

U.S. Navy. (2005). *US Navy 050320-N-5884M-001 Sailors from all departments aboard the Nimitz-class aircraft carrier USS Dwight D. Eisenhower (CVN 69) participate in a Foreign Object Damage (FOD) walk down* [Photograph]. Accessed at http://commons.wikimedia.org/wiki/File:US_Navy_050320-N-5884M-001_Sailors_from_all_departments_aboard_the_Nimitz-class_aircraft_carrier_USS_Dwight_D._Eisenhower_(CVN_69)_participate_in_a_Foreign_Object_Damage_(FOD)_walk_down.jpg on November 6, 2013.

van der Werf, G. (1997). Differences in school and instruction characteristics between high-, average-, and low-effective schools. *School Effectiveness and School Improvement, 8*(4), 430–448.

Walberg, H. J. (1984). Improving the productivity of America's schools. *Educational Leadership, 41*(8), 19–27.

Walberg, H. J. (1999). Productive teaching. In H. C. Waxman & H. J. Walberg (Eds.), *New directions for teaching practice and research* (pp. 75–104). Berkeley, CA: McCutchan.

Wang, M. C., Haertel, G. D., & Walberg, H. J. (1993). Toward a knowledge base for school learning. *Review of Educational Research, 63*(3), 249–294.

Weick, K. E., & Sutcliffe, K. M. (2007). *Managing the unexpected: Resilient performance in an age of uncertainty* (2nd ed.). San Francisco: Jossey-Bass.

Weick, K. E., Sutcliffe, K. M., & Obstfeld, D. (1999). Organizing for high reliability: Processes of collective mindfulness. *Research in Organizational Behavior, 1*, 81–123.

Wilkins, J. L. M. (1997). *Modeling correlates of problem-solving skills: Effects of opportunity-to-learn on the attainment of higher-order thinking skills in mathematics.* Unpublished doctoral dissertation, University of Illinois at Urbana-Champaign. (UMI No. 9732288)

Wing, R. R., Tate, D. F., Gorin, A. A., Raynor, H. A., & Fava, J. L. (2006). A self-regulation program for maintenance of weight loss. *New England Journal of Medicine, 355*, 1563–1571.

Wright, S. P., Horn, S. P., & Sanders, W. L. (1997). Teacher and classroom context effects on student achievement: Implications for teacher education. *Journal of Personnel Evaluation in Education, 11*, 57–67.

Index

A

Ambady, N., 47
Art and Science of Teaching, The (Marzano), 46, 47–48

B

Beck, I., 71
Bellamy, G. T., 1
Boyer, E., 108
Building Background Knowledge for Academic Achievement (Marzano), 73

C

Carey, T., 91
Carifio, J., 91
Carroll, J., 107
Classroom Assessment and Grading That Work (Marzano), 107
cognitive skills, 74, 75
Common Core State Standards Initiative, 69–70
competency-based education (level 5), 4, 83
     critical commitments, 107–112
     lagging indicators, 112–115
     leading indicators, 101
     long-form leading indicator surveys, 102–107
     quick data for, 115–117
     report cards, 108–112
     resources for, 117–118
     short-form leading indicator survey, 101–102
     time requirements, eliminating, 107–108
conative skills, 74, 75
Coulter, G., 1
Crawford, L., 1
credits, 107–108
criterion scores, 5, 121
critical commitments

for competency-based education (level 5), 107–112
for guaranteed and viable curriculum (level 3), 69–75
for safe and collaborative culture (level 1), 27–28
for standards-referenced reporting (level 4), 89–94
for teaching (instruction) effectiveness (level 2), 46–50
implementing, 6
culture, safe and collaborative (level 1). *See* safe and collaborative culture (level 1)
curriculum, guaranteed and viable (level 3).
     See guaranteed and viable curriculum (level 3)

D

data
     collection, level-appropriate, 11
     See also quick data, types of
developmental scale, 49
DuFour, R., 27, 89

E

Effective Supervision (Marzano), 46

F

feedback, 11
First International Mathematics Study (FIMS), 69
Formative Assessment and Standards-Based Grading (Marzano), 91, 108

G

grade levels, 107
guaranteed and viable curriculum, 4
     continuous monitoring, 70

critical commitments, 69–75
direct instruction in knowledge application and
    metacognitive skills, 73–75
lagging indicators, 75–78
leading indicators, 57
long-form leading indicator surveys, 58–69
quick data for, 78–81
resources for, 81–82
short-form leading indicator survey, 57–58
vocabulary program, comprehensive, 70–73

H

Hattie, J., 2–3
hierarchy of school factors, 2–4
high reliability organizations (HROs), defined, 1
high reliability schools (HRS)
    creating, 1–5
    critical commitments, implementing, 6
    guidelines, 119–122
    hierarchy of school factors, 2–4
    leading and lagging indicators, 4–6
    levels of operation for, 4
    monitoring performance, 6–11
    process, 13
*High School: A Report on Secondary Education in
    America* (Boyer), 108
Hoegh, J. K., 69

I

International Association for the Evaluation of
    Educational Achievement, 69

K

knowledge application, 73–75

L

lagging indicators. *See* leading and lagging indicators
Latham, G., 11
leading and lagging indicators
    cutoff scores, setting, 5
    for competency-based education (level 5),
        101–107, 112–115
    for guaranteed and viable curriculum (level 3),
        58–69, 75–78
    for safe and collaborative culture (level 1), 15–27
    for standards-referenced reporting (level 4),
        83–89, 94–97
    for teaching (instruction) effectiveness (level 2),
        37–46, 50–53

percentage approach, 5
purpose of, 4–5
selecting, 120
level 1. *See* safe and collaborative culture (level 1)
level 2. *See* teaching (instruction) effectiveness
    (level 2)
level 3. *See* guaranteed and viable curriculum (level 3)
level 4. *See* standards-referenced reporting (level 4)
level 5. *See* competency-based education (level 5)
Locke, E., 11

M

Marshall, L., 1
Marzano, R. J., 6, 27, 46, 69, 70, 71, 73, 89, 91, 107,
    108
Marzano Research, 6
McKeown, M., 71
measurement topics, 83
metacognitive skills, 73–75
monitoring performance, 6–11

O

Obstfeld, D., 1
opportunity to learn (OTL), 69

P

performance, monitoring, 6–11
Pritchett, H. S., 108–108
professional learning communities (PLCs), 27–28
proficiency scales, 89–94

Q

quick data, types of
    easy-to-collect quantitative data, 10, 34, 54–55,
        80, 98, 116–117
    examples, 35, 55–56, 80–81, 98–99, 117
    for competency-based education (level 5),
        115–117
    for guaranteed and viable curriculum (level 3),
        78–81
    for safe and collaborative culture (level 1), 33–35
    for standards-referenced reporting (level 4),
        97–99
    for teaching (instruction) effectiveness (level 2),
        53–56
    quick conversations, 8–9, 33, 53–54, 78–79,
        97–98, 115–116
    quick observations, 9–10, 33–34, 54, 79, 98, 116

R

report cards
    competency-based education (level 5), 108–112
    standards-referenced reporting (level 4), 98–94
Rosenthal, R., 47
rubrics, 89–90

S

safe and collaborative culture, 4
    critical commitments, 27–28
    lagging indicators, 28–32
    leading indicators, 15
    long-form leading indicator surveys, 16–27
    quick data for, 33–35
    resources for, 35
    short-form leading indicator survey, 15–16
school effectiveness, research on, 2
Second International Mathematics Study (SIMS), 69
semantic clusters, 71–72
Simms, J. A., 69
standards-based education. *See* competency-based
    education (level 5)
standards-referenced reporting (level 4), 4
    critical commitments, 89–94
    lagging indicators, 94–97
    leading indicators, 83
    long-form leading indicator surveys, 84–89
    proficiency scales, 89–94
    quick data for, 97–99
    resources for, 99
    short-form leading indicator survey, 83–84
Stringfield, S., 1–2
Strong, M., 119
student performance (achievement)
    influence of principals on, 27–28
    factors that affect, 2–3
Sutcliffe, K., 1

T

teacher evaluation, purposes of, 46
teacher evaluation system
    comprehensive and specific, 46–48
    developmental scale, 49
    teacher growth, support for, 50
Teaching Basic and Advanced Vocabulary (Marzano),
    71
teaching (instruction) effectiveness (level 2), 4
    critical commitments, 46–50
    lagging indicators, 50–53
    leading indicators, 37
    long-form leading indicator surveys, 38–46
    quick data for, 53–56
    resources for, 56
    short-form leading indicator survey, 37–38
Tier 1 and Tier 2 terms, 71–73
Tier 3 terms, 73, 74

U

U.S. Navy, FOD walks, 7
*Using Common Core Standards to Enhance Classroom
    Instruction and Assessment* (Marzano), 91

V

vocabulary program, comprehensive, 70–73

W

Weick, K., 1
What Works in Schools (Marzano), 69, 70

Y

Yanoski, D. C., 69

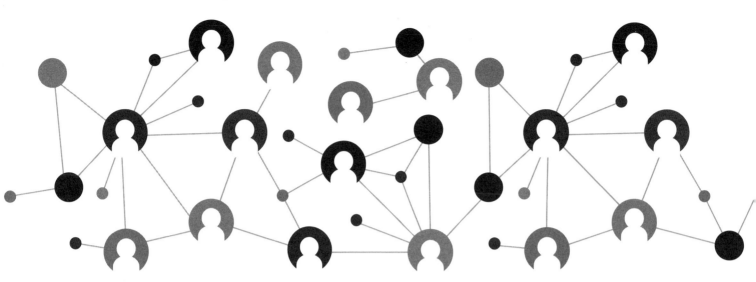

JOIN THE HRS NETWORK

An exclusive membership for schools and districts

Schools and districts who join the HRS Network will:

- Gain access to over 100 resources for implementing the five levels of reliability.

- Develop expertise through special HRS services and professional development.

- Receive invitations to the annual members-only HRS conference.

 **MARZANO** Research

Learn more!
marazanoresearch.com/HRSNetwork

Take the next step in school reform